The City of
Our God

A Vision of Love

AMY FLEMING

**For my beautiful daughter, Cora
and for the Bride**

"God is our refuge and strength,
A very present help in trouble.
Therefore we will not fear,
Even though the earth be removed,
And though the mountains be carried into the midst of
the sea;
Though the waters roar *and* be troubled,
Though the mountains shake with its swelling.

There is a river whose streams shall make glad the city
of God,
The holy *place* of the tabernacle of the Most High.
God *is* in the midst of her, she shall not be moved;
God shall help her, just at the break of dawn.
The nations raged, the kingdoms were moved;
He uttered His voice, the earth melted.

The Lord of hosts *is* with us;
The God of Jacob *is* our refuge.

Come, behold the works of the Lord,
Who has made desolations in the earth.
He makes wars cease to the end of the earth;
He breaks the bow and cuts the spear in two;
He burns the chariot in the fire.

Be still, and know that I *am* God;
I will be exalted among nations,
I will be exalted in the earth!

The Lord of hosts *is* with us;
The God of Jacob *is* our refuge."

-David
(Psalm 46)

Dear Reader,

One weekend in January of 2007, I was visiting a dear friend's house. Pat is a powerful intercessor. We were sitting in her house, praying, when we felt the presence of God hit us in unbelievable realness. He proceeded to show us a vision– at the exact same time– of a city nestled within the hillside. He went into detail about the city and the tents where we would stay. We compared notes which matched exactly.

Although her vision stopped after that day, mine continued for three more months. Almost every day, the Lord would place me in a very deep sleep. There, He would pick up where He left off the day before, showing me His very heart in the secret place of my dreams. This is the journal I kept during those three months of everything I experienced.

For those of you who have never met Him, I pray that this book will be a wonderful introduction to our Lord. (Please keep in mind as you read that the "Bride" represents true believers as a whole, who will forever live to love Jesus.) For those who already know Him, I pray that you will gain new insight into how much He loves you.

You will see that my character in this book represents the Bride of Christ. Please don't forget that. I pray that the Lord will richly bless you as He so richly has blessed my life with this beautiful dream of Him. After all, this dream is yours, as well.

Much love,
Amy

CHAPTER 1

THE BATTLE SCENE

The angels hoisted me up and tightened the invisible stirrups. The huge, white horse grunted and nodded. The small group of blonde angels patted and petted the beautiful stallion as it *neigh* back to them. They looked like angels straight out of Michelangelo's art. "May I ask you a question?" I said meekly.

"Yes," the one nearest his nose said.

"Why no saddle and why are there no reigns?"

They looked at the beauty as if he could have answered himself and said, "He has an angel's spirit. He will move perfectly to the will of the Spirit. You will not need reigns, because you will move as one on the battlefield."

I nodded. The soon-to-be battlefield was aglow in the rising morning as we awaited the orders. The smell of wet dirt was all around as the few of us who were on horses steadied ourselves. The horses anxiously stomped and kicked at the mud. I looked over in amazement to see all the foot soldiers on my right. I could make out the archangel Michael on the far right. We were both on the front lines. He did not acknowledge me, but was counting the cost ahead of him. He was dressed in full armor. Between he and I was the most beautiful, smiling face– my Lord Jesus'. From about 50 feet away, He smiled reassuringly and winked at me.

I took a deep breath as He pointed His sword and gave the signal. At once, we were off and in no more than ten seconds, the demonic army became visible and met our band in force. Some of the dark angels were unarmored and some armed with small, chiseled arrows. The arrows looked as if they had been broken. They were almost useless. *Used* weapons. They clawed and bit us as we cut them through. I had to bend low to nab them as they tried to bite at my horse. Each devil looked distinctively different.

The angels were right, the horse acted as if his legs were my legs and we scurried and swayed in one accord. I felt like a centaur. As we pushed through, my small battalion started catching up to me. I heard the Lord yell to me. I looked over. He was fighting on foot with His massive sword. He looked like He was actually *enjoying* this very easy battle. "Amy! Take the city!" He yelled.

Just in front of me was an ancient city made entirely of stone houses with a stone gate around it. The gate and everything in it was a sand color. I gave a signal to my troops, all the brave women on horseback, and we pushed through with greater speed and strength then a band of wild horses would have.

Covering the city was a hologram of a humongous giant, twice the size of the entire city, starting to stand up from a frontal laying position. I found myself with reigns in hand. At the same time, I pulled back on them with all my might. My little army stopped cold around me and gazed up in terror. I did not know how to take this city! I did not know how to fight this giant. Who did I think I was? I could not pull my brave women into that. In that same second, I blacked out, probably from a blow to the head by the enemy.

THE TREE

When I opened my eyes, I was holding onto my knees. My wet, straggly hair limply fell in front of my face as I looked up. I was under a tree. It looked like a willow tree. It was dense and covered me on all sides. I sat up against the trunk of it. The archangel, Michael, was guarding it from just outside it's umbrella of leaves. He was standing directly in front of me with his back turned. I looked at his beautiful sandals, which were the only part of him that was perfectly visible. Another set of feet walked towards him on our left. I knew exactly who this was by the uneven nail prints in his feet. "Have you come to speak to the general?" Michael asked with no emotion.

"No, I have come to talk with my friend." With that, He took off a dirty, short, outer garment and put on a longer one that was thicker. The tree dripped of honey all around me [1]. I could not figure out the source. Some of it was dripping on me, but most ran down the leaves of the tree onto the ground. He parted back the tree limbs like a curtain. I could see His face. It was so sweet and gentle. "Do you want to talk to me?" He asked.

"Not really." I said in severe disappointment of myself. Never have I ever felt that low and discouraged. The tears were just dripping directly from my eyes to my knees, skipping my cheeks.

"Can I sit by you?" He asked. I nodded. He sat down on the ground on my right. Already I felt lighter, but the sense of wanting to pout was still inside of me.

"Why did you let me go into the battle, knowing that I would pull back like that?" I asked angrily.

"I hoped you would surprise me," He said smiling.

"Lord, I can never surprise you."

He paused. "I want to show you something..." He reached with his right hand into a pocket under His outer garment. He pulled out a red balloon. I was a surprised for some reason that He even had pockets.

"Are you going to try to cheer me up with balloon animals?" I replied freshly.

"No..." He laughed. "*This* is the demonic stronghold," He said, holding up the deflated balloon. Then He started blowing the balloon up until it almost popped. He pinched the nozzle with His fingers and pointed to the huge balloon. "*This* is what it did to itself when it saw you coming." He reached in His pocket one more time to pull out a large nail that looked ancient. He popped the balloon with the nail. I jumped. "Now wasn't that easy?"

I nodded, starting to get the revelation. "You see," He continued, "right when you are on the verge of winning a battle, the enemy rears itself up to scare you. But that makes him an easy target because he *shows* himself and you know exactly who he is and where he is."

Things do get worse right before you take the victory, I thought to myself.

I looked at Him with complete understanding. "There's something more we have to do here," He said. An angel's feminine hands appeared on the left of me holding a rainbow colored bowl filled half way with water. On its edge, it had a clean cloth. Her hands held my upper chest and back as I reclined a little. The Lord lifted my left foot in the air. Taking a very sharp instrument, He cut slightly into my inner ankle. It was painful. My ankle started dripping dark-red blood. My hands gripped to the angel's hand holding my upper chest, as I winced.

A chip like you would see in a computer came out with the Lord's coaxing. He held the square, silver thing up and examined it. It was about the size of a nickel and had jagged lines etched into it. He dropped it in the water bowl with a *ting*. "Your identity." He told me. "Everything that your genes tell you you are, everything everyone else told you

you are, and everything you thought you were– gone." He pressed His palm onto my ankle and pulled it back to reveal no wound. But it still hurt.

THE JOURNEY

When I was finally better, He helped me up with His hand and said, "I see no defeat here...come a way with me."[2] He parted the leaf curtain again and a huge area like a ballroom appeared. It was so big, I couldn't even see walls- they were so far away. It seemed dark and deserted, like a ballroom shut up except for major events. There was a crystal floor. I stepped onto it and slid a little. He joined me and we slid around the floor and laughed together. We just had that moment for no other reason other than we just love to be together. In our laughter, I could hear someone calling me. Jesus watched me with a smile on His face as I stepped curiously toward the voice.

"Amy!" a groggy voice muttered out of darkness, "I see us walking up a hill towards a man. We thought at first was Jesus, but it's an angel..."

No sooner than I heard my dear friend Pat say the word "walking" that I started having the same vision she was. Suddenly, there we were, on the beautiful green hills, just emerging from a dense wood. As we got closer to the top of a large hill, we parted hands. We had been holding hands to balance ourselves on the uneven terrain.

I started to see the crest of a man's head. Then, he was in plain view. He stepped to our right and motioned his hand (like an usher shows you your seat) to show us what lay in front of us. It was a beautiful, modern-looking city that was completely nestled within the green hills. It was an absolutely beautiful, bright white.

The houses were crystal and not one that I could see had glass in the windows. There was one sky scraper that I knew instinctively was an administration building. What compelled me the most is the feeling deep inside me that the Tabernacle of David was somewhere in there. I had to get to it! My heart was aching for it.

I thought about just sliding down the hill, but knew I would get really hurt. I was also very concerned about my older traveling companion sliding down. "Amy! He's showing us into an elevator!" cried out Pat. I looked over to our right to see the angel ushering us into an elevator. It was glass and went straight down the side of the hill and stopped at the gate of the city.

We were immediately in the city upon getting off the elevator. We walked a few steps into the beautiful place slowly. We were on a narrow road that had two-story houses that butt up right next to it. Everything was so bright that my eyes were hurting. I looked down at my feet. I was walking on pretty bricks that made up the streets. They were white like frosted glass and on each of them was a name. They were all written in different languages. I didn't see any English names where I was standing, so I couldn't read any of them. I asked the Lord what they were. He pressed on my heart that these bricks were the names of the saints that had gone before me, paving the way I should go.

I looked up and saw a woman on the second story of a white building. She was shaking out a white rug, which seemed to have dust coming off of it in the sunlight. I looked closer and thought it might be glitter until it came at almost eye-level to me. The dust was actually beautifully cut diamonds! I caught them in a leather satchel that hung at my waist and gathered up what I could that fell to the ground. *Doesn't she know where I come from how valuable these are?* I thought as I tucked them away to give to someone back home.

THE PARK

We looked straight ahead. About 15 feet away, was a park with a bench right at the "entrance" of it. The park was surrounded by the street that forked off from the entrance of the park. There were buildings everywhere except in the park. The buildings were not obtrusive, though. They were all nicely spaced, none being more than two stories. All of them were a white color.

We went and sat down. To me, the bench looked black and iron. I took off my hiking boots that laced up almost to my knees. I was wearing dark, green khaki shorts that were some-what rolled up. I had on a short-sleeve, linen shirt. My hair was cut short and was sweaty. I had been on this hike for a while.

A long stem with a flower on the end arose from the soft, green grass. It grew instantly there beside me to the right of the bench. It seemed to look at me as it's bud opened and lean towards my face. I smelled the sweet fragrance of rose mixed with jasmine. It was a hot pink- almost red. It looked a lot like the kind of flowers you see on a dogwood tree, but more petals. It was not only alive, it was moving and growing before my eyes.

Pat cried out, "Oh! I see someone. I think it's a servant... It's Steven!" I looked up and standing in front of Pat was a tall man who held out his hand. In it was a tiny, gold treasure chest. Pat saw the little treasure chest as bread and ate it. He bent down towards her and changed her shoes and washed her feet. She was throughly enjoying it, although it disgusted me a little. I was hoping he would not do the same to me. He put lambs wool slippers on her that belted up high to the middle of her calf like a boot.

I asked for high heel boots so I could walk around the city, but was flat-out denied. As Steven was tending to Pat's feet, he looked up at me. "You're seeing me how I looked in

17

the flesh." He said still working. His front teeth overlapped each other a little and his face was very thin. He had high cheek bones and dark, short hair.

I thought, *very interesting...* but I had an agenda and couldn't be bothered with details at that point. "Where is my Lord?" I asked dismissing him quickly. I looked closer as he turned towards his work again. I looked at him hard, searching for an answer. I thought I would cover all the bases and asked, "Are *you* my Lord?"

"No, Amy, you think that because here everyone has the same mannerisms as He, but I am *not* the Lord."

"Tell me where He is.[3]"

"You must rest now." I couldn't believe or accept His answer.

He put gold bands around our heads, laying them around our foreheads and closing them into a circle in the back. They were an absolutely perfect length to go all the way around our heads. The gold shined in the sun. It felt a little tight.

"Please! I must find Him! Tell me!" I demanded. He ignored me as Pat sat with her head back in blissful ignorance.

I slipped on some kind of shoe that was like a low, soft slipper he passed to me. I grabbed his arm as he got up. "Please! Where is He?"

"He must come to *you* this time, Amy." I let him go. The atmosphere turned to dusk and I could feel a soft, gauzy fabric brushing up against me. Ahead of me, as if the tent had actually passed by me, were two beautiful tents suspended from nothing. They hung about fifty feet from us. They were an off-white, veil-like fabric that hung in a small clearing of the park behind and to the right of the bench.

We raced toward our temporary homes. "There's one for each of us!" I heard Pat coo. We had to leave everything at that bench we brought with us. I kept trying to walk towards the tents, and kept getting pulled back and told to leave something else.

CHAPTER 2

THE CHAMBER

Pat buzzed in on the tent on the right- each of us instinctively knowing our tent from the other. There was a huge satin pillow that encompassed the majority of the gorgeous, circular tent. I saw Pat plop down immediately through the two layers of veil between us and fall asleep. Before she dozed, she yelled to me- which really wasn't necessary- that there were pomegranates and a bowl of honey on a table for us to eat.[4]

We could both feel the gold band Steven put on us sink into our heads. It slid down into our bodies like it was going down a main artery to our hearts. There, I could see the band wind around our hearts until our hearts started turning gold. It seemed like it was melting into us and becoming part of us. I lay down finally and saw that our old tv from when I was a little girl was lying in front of me on it's side. I could view it lying down on my side. There was a man sitting at a desk on the screen, droning on about the second coming and so forth. I could turn that tv on and off at will and see exactly what I needed to hear. I turned it off and tried to rest.

As I was starting to nod off, a lovely breeze came by and with it a whisper, "*I killed your giant. I see no defeat here. I see no defeat here.*" The words of the Lord beat into me like a jogger on a sidewalk. "Amy..." The whisper continued. I tried to get up three times to see what I was suppose to be shown, but couldn't. I was exhausted like a drug had been given to me. "Rest now..." the voice soothed.

THE WARRIOR

Finally, after many hours, my strength started to come back to me. "Amy...come away with me." I parted the veil of the tent and saw my Lord with a gold crown on with encrusted with jewels. He looked so handsome! He took my hand. I looked down and saw I wore a beautiful white satin gown that hung loosely on me. My hair had grown long again and was light brown and wavy. I was clean and my skin felt like a baby's- with no freckles. The dress had a tucked bodice and a long, feather-light, pink jacket that went over top.

It was dark outside.

He led me to a hill overlooking a battleground. He waved His hand in front of us and a vision appeared before me of a battle. There was one very muscular, well-equipped man standing in the middle of hundreds of enemies attacking him. He was so fast that he defeated every demon that came towards him in one single blow each. He continued until all of them were dead. When killed, they disappeared like water sinking into the ground.

The Lord said, "Behold, one of David's mighty men!"[5] The man looked up at me. It was my husband! He looked like he had when I met him ten years ago. His hair was long and tied back, but lighter than I remembered it, and his arms were sculpted. He had on a light-weight vest of armor and was bleeding from flesh wounds all over him. He looked tired.

The Lord spoke from the deep recesses of my heart. "You have been guilt ridden over getting married this whole time because you thought you could do more for Me single. You considered it a weakness for you to be married and have a family. Because of this, you have not fully taken on the responsibility of him. He is wounded, go to him."

I ran as fast as I could to him down that hill. I had not interceded like I should have for him, the Lord was right. All of it was right. On contact, he spun me around like he had missed me. He knelt down and held my hands. He moved my hands and placed them over his head. Oil dripped quickly from my hands and covered him all over like vitamin E.

I walked back to the Lord on the hill. He clasped my hand to steady me. I was still weak from the journey. He could feel I wanted to see more of the city, but He told me reassuringly, "You cannot leave the tent area without Pat. You both have to experience it together because you will see with different view points. I need both of my eyes to make up my vision." I didn't mind having to go with Pat (although I could hardly wait for her). She had been one of my spiritual mothers. There was a great bond there that only comes with hard intercession for each other and with each other. We were Naomi and Ruth.

The next second, I was waking up on my satin pillow in my tent. It couldn't have been a dream, I reasoned to myself, because I was wearing the same dress. Pat slept deeply in the next tent with her back towards me, her red hair moving softly in the breeze. I marveled at the energy she even exuded in her sleep. She tossed and turned and tore up the bed she was in as she dreamed. She always seemed at least fifty years younger than she was. Spunky was a good word for her. I chuckled to myself as I drifted off.

(Pat was having a lovely dream which she later told me about. She found herself in the upper room. We were all sitting around a table like the one painted time and again of the last supper. But the atmosphere was dynamically different. The disciples were there and so were many of the intercessors she knew. We were all wearing white, heather wreathes around our heads. The Lord Jesus was sitting in the middle of all of us and was able to give each of us undivided attention somehow. He was wearing a gold, heather wreath around his head and a big grin. He did not look stressed or concerned. He looked totally in his element and totally satisfied.)

OH! THE JEWELRY!

The breeze came again in the middle of feverish dreams I cannot remember. My whole body ached with the pressure of conviction. Just being in this holy place, made my heart grieve for my sinful self. I could hear Him whispering again as the tent whisked around my face. "Amy..." I looked towards my feet, and there the Lord stood, just beyond the entrance of the tent. I scrambled towards Him on all fours.

Without speaking, He lay out a woven mat of all different colors at the entrance way. [6] He knelt at the opening and moved His seemingly empty hands over the mat like He was pouring something out of them. On the mat, appeared a half dozen or more gold bracelets, each with different widths. Some were at least an inch wide, and some were only a centimeter. They were like bangles, but all a beautiful, brilliant gold. "For you..." He said. I was hesitant to take them, fearing it was a test of some sort to see if I was materialistic, but there was something about those bracelets and something about His eyes, that invited me to at least try them on.

I stacked the majority of them on my left arm, ending with the thickest of them towards my wrist. Only *one* I placed on my right arm and it was a medium width. "These bracelets are yours. They represent the gifts I have given you. They represent your calling." I looked up at Him. Only in the last few weeks had God given me a few clues to what He was going to do with my life. The past 28 years had only been a relentless pursuit of dying to Him. I raised my left arm up and down, expecting to hear the bracelets each time, but they were silent, even when clanging to each other.

"I'm glad you like them." He said with joy and almost bashfulness on His face. I really did. They seemed to become part of me instantly. He turned and got up to leave.

He walked a few steps away from the tent and vanished. I stood up, panic driven. I screamed out for him like a child who had a nightmare. "Jesus! Don't leave me! I need you!" He instantly appeared again and walked over to me casually.

"I will never leave you or forsake you, Amy." [7] He spoke from somewhere deep within me, "Give me your fear of losing Me once and for all. Your giant is fear and I have already defeated him." He continued audibly, "Even when you cannot see me, I am still here with you." But I clung to Him and would not let Him go. [8]

We knelt down by the mat where my bracelets had been. "Amy, do you love Me more than your calling?" Although I absolutely loved my new bracelets that represented my calling in life, I immediately tried to rip them off and throw them at His feet.

"Of course!" I said, "Take them! Without you, there is nothing!" Suddenly, I could hear the sound of the bracelets clanging against each other. They were still on my arms. "Always remember this lesson." I knew every time I hear the clanging of the bracelets, every time my gifts would work together, I would remember.

PAT'S GIFTS

The next second, I found myself waking up on my satin pillow again looking around. "He must have had to knock me out so He could leave..." I said out loud. I heard the breathing of Pat next door to me again, her steady rhythm brought such calm to me.

A beautiful blond woman in her thirties stood at the entrance to her tent and Pat suddenly sat up on her pillow and greeted her jovially. The woman smiled and came in with an old-fashioned sewing box that unfolded like an accordion on both sides.

"Here's the jewelry I told you I wanted to go through with you, Pat," she said as she lay it down on the pillow with Pat sitting beside her. She kept all the jewelry in individual zip-lock bags and put them in piles. She took out one beautiful piece after another. She told Pat she could have a beautiful light pink gemstone ring which Pat happily put on her ring finger. I stood outside the entrance to Pat's tent and watched the two merry women.

"And what are you doing here, Ms Amy? You don't even like jewelry." She teased me.

"I like these," I said showing her my new bracelets.

"Oh, my..." she said in amazement, recognizing at once what they represented. "Look-y, look-y what I got!" she said showing off her new ring to me, her eyes sparkling with youth.

"That's really pretty," I said wide-eyed.

"This is for you," the pretty, blonde lady said, lifting up a gorgeous necklace to me. It was the same kind of light pink stone as Pat's ring, but much bigger and a tear-drop shape. I put it on immediately. It looked perfect with my pink jacket and white gown. "And one for your forehead," she said handing me an identical one to wear around my head like I had worn the gold band. The stone hit me just between the eyes, but was not heavy like I thought it would be. The blonde lady gathered up all the little bags of jewelry, stuffed them in her case and stood up.

"I will come play with you again sometime," she said and left us. I kinda felt sorry for Pat because I had gotten much bigger jewelry than she. She then looked up and from behind her wavy bob of red hair were the biggest ruby earrings I had ever seen.

"The light pink represents the intercessory spirit I have given you two," the Spirit of the Lord burned within me. He continued, "The red ruby earrings on Pat represent prophecy."

I felt so overwhelmed, still standing in her entrance way, not sure if I could go in or not. "Oh, Pat," I sniffled. She welcomed me in like a mother to her little child. "I'm having such a hard time..." I sat down next to her on her gigantic pillow as the tears dripped down.

"God is doing a deep, deep work in you, child," she said in a deeper voice than usual.

"I feel like my heart is bleeding, it's so full." I could actually feel the thick consistency of blood ooze out of my pores where my heart was and drip all over my clothes, but I could not see it. I stood up and walked towards her vanity table. I looked around in awe of how much more she had in her tent than me.

There was the vanity with perfume on it and a small, white dresser with a mirror. She also had her little table with refreshments on it on the far side of where I was standing. Between the vanity and the little dresser was a small, silver sink which I leaned over, my back towards her, to catch all my tears. "I know I will love Him more after this experience, but I don't see how. My heart cannot possibly take any more."

"Your heart will explode with love for Him, Amy. But that love will be passed forth to everyone else." She moved her hand on the pillow, smoothing it out. Her hand fell into one of the tucks of the pillow and pulled out a little baggy with diamond earrings inside. The earrings looked as if you could put them together and they would make a complete firework. "The lady! She must have left this. Go run and find her, Amy!"

"I can go?"

"Yes! Hurry up!"

I ran out of the tent, the earrings in hand. *This could be a perfect opportunity to see a little more of the city.* However, not more than 20 feet from the tents, I remembered the voice of the Lord. It was like thunder from Heaven, "You cannot leave the tents without Pat."

I spun around, but it was too late, the earth opened up to drop me into a hole just big enough to fit my small body. There was black slime all around me, very close to me.

A cover that looked like a street grate for water overflow was put directly over my head. I rattled the bars in protest. Surely nothing like this could exist in the City of God!

"Father!" I cried out. "Jesus! Lift me out of here!" The grate was thrown open as if it had never been bolted on and the mighty arm of the Lord lifted me out. [9]

He ran me back to the tents as I angrily said, "You gave me no 'check' in my spirit about going out! You could have reminded me of your words! I thought You meant that I *couldn't* leave the tents without Pat- not *shouldn't*!" I looked down at my gown- spotless. How could this be?

My argument was to no avail. I was guilty. "You cannot disobey me, Amy. One wrong move and you can become enslaved again." I tried to catch my breath in the entrance of my tent. We kneeled there on the multi-colored rug once more. He put His hand above my heart and branded me with an oval stamp-looking tool. I could feel the searing of the heat as smoke lightly went up. "Put My words as a seal upon your heart [10]." Days later I would remember to read it. In an oval were the Hebrew words for "My Word".

He handed me back the earrings. "These are Pat's." I could feel the Spirit of God burn within me. "They represent evangelism. She will sometimes need to change into them." Then He vanished.

THE RETURN OF THE EARRINGS

"Did you find her?" Pat called out oblivious from the tent beside me. I rolled my eyes and walked towards her entrance.

"No." I couldn't believe she had missed all of that. "But I saw Jesus. He said these are yours." I handed her the diamond earrings.

"I thought so," she said and hummed merrily as she got up and put them on her vanity.

"There's something I didn't tell you... I can't leave the tents without you."

"Why didn't you tell me this?" She sounded defensive.

"I didn't think it was important at the time..."

"Well, it is!" She said gruffly. "I've been covering your butt in prayer this whole time– you better not leave without me!" That was a little humbling.

FINDING THE LOVER

I heard an angel calling me into my tent, her voice singing to me, "Amy! It's time to get ready to go out from here!"

I ran back to my tent, and just as I left, a beautiful angel appeared in Pat's tent to get her ready as well. My angel's face was simple and pale and looked young, like she was in her early 20's. She had dark hair that fell a little past her shoulders. She put on me a beautiful purple and blue gown.

Over the top of it, was the most important part it seemed, because she went very slowly with this part of the garment. It fit like a hospital gown with long sleeves which tied twice in the back. It went over my dress, but I could see the dress through it because it was a beautiful iridescent, translucent material. It was a little coarse and I realized why I had to have long sleeves on my gown. The material would have probably irritated me. It seemed to be a type of apron for a special project I was going to do. I could see bells and pomegranate seeds tied by twisted red thread at the bottom of my gown [11].

"You are going to be ministering to the Lord," she told me sing-song-y. I was so excited. When we were finished dressing, Pat and I both burst out of our tents at the same time. I was a little surprised at how she couldn't contain herself with excitement either. The angel called out to us, "Go and find Him!"

And we were off, giggling and holding hands, running as fast as we could together. There was so much joy and excitement in that moment. The air was cold, not the usual pleasant warmth. It felt damp, which was also nothing we had experienced since our arrival. It had been night since we had gotten to our tents. I didn't know if it had been hours, days, or weeks since our arrival, because of the constant night. The soil was very wet beneath our feet, and we could barely make out the grassy hills we were plunging through.

THE LOVER

In one millisecond, everything stopped. It felt as if we had run into an invisible brick wall. For when we had stomped over the last little hill in delight, we saw Him. But

He was not as all what we expected. We fell to our knees, not being able to stand. There He was. Dead. On a cross.

At the sight too horrible for words, my head sank to the ground as a low groan came out of me so horrid I thought I, too, was going to die. I banged my fists into the wet soil. Pat held onto me, trying to gather me back up, but it was useless. There was no skin on Him. I sobbed silently and without breath.

We watched as the cross was lifted slowly in the air and them turned even more slowly around by an invisible force. It was then placed gently back to the ground where it had been before. It was as if the Father had picked Him up and softly caressed Him. The Father was grieving pathetically as a parent who had just lost their child. He wanted to hold Him, but couldn't.

With only a little oxygen in me, I breathed out, "The angel told us to minister to Him. I have to go to Him."

"He's already gone, child."

"It doesn't matter. I must try to minister to Him." I used the last bits of strength I seemed to have in my body to stagger to the base of the cross, where His feet were not far from. I thought maybe it may mean something to the Father to see me try to get close to Him– some small shred of comfort to Him.

As I made my way, bits of lightning flickered around. As it did, it would light up the area. I could see in those few seconds of lighting into the past. I could see Roman soldiers. I thought I made out the women around the cross. It was hard to make anything out in those flashes, especially in the state I was in. I feared that the soldiers could see me, but I reasoned quickly to myself that it didn't matter. I was going to die there of grief anyway. I crouched down right under His feet.

Blood was not dripping down, it was pouring. It ran all over my back and hair over and over again. I must have knelt bent over like that for hours, because His blood dried and crusted into my matted hair and then kept pouring. There seemed to be no end to it, until finally Pat picked me up. The apron had been put on me to catch the blood of the Lord as it went into the back of it where it was tied. All of me was meant to be covered. Not one drop was to fall on the ground.

Pat informed me, "The men are coming to take Him away now." I could see shadows of men start to gang around Him, ready to bury Him as she led me away. I was like a zombie, staring into the distance. She led me to a pond far to the right of us. The pond was smoking into the cold air, but when I stepped into it, it felt even colder than the air was. I got the majority of the chunks of blood out of my hair.

All was going dark and I felt totally useless. I could feel some other people around me, but I couldn't really make out anyone. I was rushed into a house of some sort. It looked like it was made of rock and was very small. I then totally blacked out.

CHAPTER 3

THE BATH HOUSE

There was a marble bath tub inlaid with silver. I started gaining consciousness again as I stared blankly in the warm water of the tub. I remember vaguely the water turning red with the blood. The blood had not been cleaned entirely off of me in the lake. There were three female angels who were tending to me. Triplets. They had to keep pouring out the water and filling it up again and again to get me clean. They reminded me of friends back home who were identical twins. I felt very comforted by their presence.

Pat knelt by my tub. "We know the story," she said soothingly, "in three days there is a resurrection." But I knew no resurrection. I knew death. I knew pain. And not even that perfect sentence she spoke to me could bring comfort. This was the moment that there was no comfort. This was the moment of the cross. Pat left.

The second day in that stone room was a little more clear. There were a few pieces of furniture, like a dresser and a wash basin on the far side of the small room from where my tub was. There was also a wooden chair that looked very simple as well. On the same side of the room as the tub, there was a large window with no glass. I could see the three young angels better during the last two days, they were petite and pretty.

I didn't know exactly how they were changing the water in the tub except to dump it out the window. I also don't remember them getting me out and into the tub when doing so. It's all so very foggy because of the unbelievable and unbearable grief I was experiencing. There has never been a death or any kind of sorrow in my life that compared with what I experienced in those days.

Early, early on the third day, I awoke in a freezing cold tub. I looked down to see it filled with black water. At the same time as noticing the water, I heard footsteps. I saw in my spirit a very steep staircase going up to my room. I was on the second floor!

That explained not having any doors. There was an opening into a staircase behind me that I could make out if I twisted my neck. There was a woman, about in her fifties, coming up the staircase. She was heavy-set with black, graying hair to her shoulders. She looked worn out. I had never seen this woman before in my life.

She put her hand on her hips and looked at me. I sank into the black water so my head was only showing. She then cinched up her pants around her thigh as she sat down on the wooden chair only a foot from me. "I am Lydia, like the rich lady Lydia in the Bible. You know," she said with obvious resentment in her voice, "this is *my* house. And while you are in my house, I need to speak to you about a few things—mainly your attitude."

I turned away from her and put my mouth on the marble tub, tasting the salt of it. I could not shut her out, she kept on, "You've been moping up here for days and everyone is just tired of it. You need to pick yourself up and encourage yourself in the Lord. And furthermore..." She could not continue because the three angels appeared in the room by the window.

They ganged up on her saying, "You have no right to be here. Out! The daughter needs to grieve! You get out right now! Leave her alone!" They pushed her out with their words. An old fashioned plank door appeared and was shut in her face at the foot of the staircase. Then, one of the angels latched it like a gate so that she could not bombard me again.

"We are so sorry!" They immediately pleaded with me. "Please forgive us! Her tub is cold! Look at how black! We had to step out for a few minutes. I promise we weren't gone long. Get her out! Get the big towel, her lips are blue." I tried to reassure them as they stood me up and caught me into a white towel as big as a sheet. They wrapped it around me, sat me in the chair and then took smaller, white towels and patted my feet and arms down.

My pores were still oozing a black residue which they were sopping up in the towels. "Your body is de-toxing from all the infirmities of sin," they explained to me, even though I could not audibly ask. My eyes grew wide and fearful. I felt a contraction as if giving birth. They took a silver bed pan and placed it under me. Bright orange toxins flooded out of me in one second. "It's okay, this is good," they said as the good nurses they were.

The towels were turning gray from the black of my pores and I muttered out my first words in three days, "I'm sorry..."

They shook their heads with tearful eyes as if to say, "Oh please, don't be..." I could hardly hold my head up. It kept flopping from one side to the other shoulder. As I was losing consciousness again, I could feel them throw huge furs on top of me to pick up my body temperature. [12]

"Princess, let me get this arm... Your highness, I know you don't like me touching your feet, I'm almost done..."

They spoke quietly to me. I knew why they were taking care of me then. They thought I was royalty. I was afraid to tell them they had the wrong person, because I so needed their help, but I started to try to. Then, one of them interrupted my thoughts by a sweet song that went like this:

"I will tell you a story of a King,
Who fell in love with a pauper girl.
Who could not love.
But it only took one touch
from the King
to make her royalty.
Many stories have told of love,
but none can compare
With the King of Kings,
The Great I Am
and the little pauper girl."

One of them, held my chin and knelt in front of me. She looked hard into my vacant eyes and smiled. "It's almost done. I see you have dove's eyes [13]." Doves only see one direction at a time. At that moment, there was only one direction I could see, my Lord, my Love, on the cross. A sudden surge of healing flooded into me. I felt like I was not going to die. I just felt very weary like I had been sick and in bed a long time.

They stood me up and dressed me in beautiful, blue high heels. The straps went over close to the toe and seemed to be latched on by a magnet. They put a long, blue, silk skirt on me that pleated in the back. I begged them not to, because I thought I would stain these beautiful clothes, but they commented that it didn't matter at this point. Then, they put a silk, dark brown top with no sleeves on me, because I suddenly felt warm again. It reminded me of lady in waiting clothes.

THE SUNRISE

They left, and so did the tub, instantly. The room was clean and was beginning to become a little lighter. The door was still latched and undisturbed. I walked over to the large window, feeling a foot taller in those shoes. The window went from my knees to my forehead. I folded my arms above my head and leaned against the top of the window.

I could see the sun trying to rise. The sky was a beautiful pink and the streets were lit for the first time since our arrival to the park tents. I could see the park from my window and wondered if this was the window the lady had shook the diamonds from when we arrived here.

I could see the bench as well, but it was turned around to face the sunrise ahead on the horizon. I could make out Pat sitting there, gently rocking herself, waiting for the morning to come. I saw a street sweeper. He stopped and looked up at me, resting his chin on the broom handle. I turned away from the window as I felt Pat speak into my spirit, "Everyone who goes into ministry has to go through this. They all have to go through the cross."

I nodded my head, thinking, "How can one have a ministry worth anything without the revelation of the cross?"

As I pondered these thoughts, the door burst open. Light sprayed into the room so powerfully that it had *wind*! My garments were turned to a white silk and my hair was instantly flowing with a white veil that was secured with four clips at the base of my scalp. I winced in agony for my eyes. My eyes adjusted a little and there He was! The resurrected Lord standing in the doorway. I flung myself to Him in a shriek of delight. I held onto Him until He pulled me away a little to look at me. I was crying out with joy.

LEAVING THE BATH HOUSE

I held onto His arm as we descended the steep, stone staircase to where there was a small living area, flooded with people. They were all smiling, anxious to see us. I recognized the lady who falsely called herself Lydia. I also saw Pat at the bottom of the stairs. Jesus let go of me for a moment to go speak quietly to the Lydia lady and then came immediately back to me. I grabbed hold of His arm ravenously. He escorted Pat and I out into the street. "Are you ready to see the city now?!" *Were we!*

We walked out to the crystal-bricked street in front of the house. I stopped dead in my tracks. "Lord, can I go thank the three angels?" He nodded in proud approval. I ran back into the house, my dress flowing almost weightlessly everywhere. I looked back only for a moment to hear a conversation between the two I had left on the street.

Jesus kissed Pat on the forehead and commented, "You did a great job with her, Pat."

"She looks 100% better thanks to you, Lord. You deserve all the praise and honor and glory."

"It's my job," He said with a twinkle in His eye, as if to say He loved it. I looked back to the steps and ran up them with a grace I do not normally possess. I found the three in the room, cleaning up the last little bit silently. They dropped everything and fell to their knees in shock when they saw me. We held hands there, all on our knees, and cried together. I kissed each of them on the head. "Thank you. I want to know your names."

"My name is Lynette."

"My name is Sophia."

"My name is Clara."

"Thank you." I said and kissed them all again on their heads. Then I left quickly, because I didn't want to *ever* leave them. But there was someone waiting for me. I flung down the steps toward the King. Pat and I walked behind Him and sang in unison with a new praise song deep from our hearts as loud as possible. We called out for everyone inside their homes to praise our Lord. I *needed* the Lord to receive all the praise and honor.

(If I was a mother, fully fed and nourished and had my small baby dying of dehydration in my arms... If someone tried to give me the water to me instead of to the baby, I would have forcefully given it to my baby. This is how I felt about giving Him all the praise. I needed and wanted none. I wanted Him to have it all.)

At last, we stopped, and He looked hard at me. "Do you want to leave me now?"

"I never want to leave You or this place. But, Lord, I am so tired."

He looked at me knowing I am only dust. "Go back to your family for a time," He said. I opened my eyes in my living room.

CHAPTER 4

THE CITY

A half a day later, I went back, arriving at some sort of bus stop only a few yards from where I had left them. I stood in a turn-around type of street where there was an enclosed glass area where people could wait for the bus. It was curved like the road it sat next to and held one long bench inside of it. Jesus and Pat were sitting there, a foot apart, having a seemingly wonderful time. Pat was swinging her feet that didn't quite touch the sidewalk beneath her.

I had on a traveling outfit that was more practical than anything else that I wore since we arrived there. A sleeve-less fluttering top, flowing skirt, heals, all in yellow silk. My hair was pulled back from my face with two mother of pearl clips. I put my arms wide out and crouched down as if to jump in the air as I yelled excitedly, "I'm back! I'm sorry to keep you waiting!"

"I didn't mind, did you?" Pat asked as Jesus chuckled like they had a secret joke between them.

I felt like a little girl at Disney World as we started out to explore the beautiful city. I got so excited, I was skipping a little ahead of them until I heard a very gentle voice say, "Don't get ahead of me, Amy." Embarrassed, I sheepishly fell back behind the Lord.

About a block away, my eyes bugged out. The Tabernacle of David! We were walking *past* it!

Pat marched beside me, taking all of the scenery in as if they each had a beautiful floral scent. She had on a robe much like the Lord's with long sleeves and a long vest that hung over top. Her vest color was a light pink, the Lord's was a light gold. Pat seemed totally in her element. Unlike me, she even dressed the part. I was always wearing clothes that looked like they were from back home. She mused at all the different buildings as if she had grown up here and had missed it. I was the obvious rookie.

I was trying to see into the Temple. On the stairs that led up it, an old man walked with a long, white beared. I thought he was a high priest. He didn't seem to see us, which was odd because we were the only other people out. As I was watching him, *bang*, I walked into a tall, black pole. My mouth was bleeding all over the place and I fell back. Jesus immediately ran over and took his sleeve to wipe all the blood up. The blood stopped quickly and He restored me with only the touch of His garment's sleeve.

As He did, He joked with me. "You're silly today. You have to keep your eyes on Me when we are walking." He paused, checking my mouth inside. He talked to me like a doctor trying to get my mind off of my ailment, "You know that Nacho Libra movie?" I laughed out loud because it seemed totally ridiculous that He watches those slap-stick movies I love so much *with* me.

I quoted the movie to Him, "Big kiss, little hug, kiss, kiss, little kiss." We both laughed. "Or Rocket Man," I said.

We sang the song from the movie together, "Close your monkey, monkey eyes..." We laughed harder. I was shocked to find Him with the same stupid sense of humor as I have.

THE TABERNACLE OF DAVID

With a last little chuckle, He looked toward the Tabernacle with it's huge pillars. "It is not in my plan to go in there right now." He looked at Pat who was shaking her head and rolling her eyes, pretending to be annoyed from the silliness we were sharing. "But, I guess we could go take a peek." He was relenting to me as a father to a small child. I bounced up and followed Him up the staircase to the inside of the huge building.

The old man had gone inside by this time. He was carrying a bowl that was rainbow striped. It looked just like the bowl from the honey tree my identity had been dropped into. He was walking to do something on the right of the building. When He saw Jesus enter and come towards Him down the aisle, He dropped the bowl and fell on His face. Jesus picked him up and put His hands on his shoulders. "Samuel. Thank you."

With that, Samuel fell back down on his face and kissed the hem of the King's garment. Jesus picked him back up again. Samuel was grieved by Jesus thanking him and cried unconsolable. "You will never know how many lives you touched by your obedience," He said. Samuel, visibly moved again, reached up to a huge table behind him and brought down one grain of sand that glittered in the light. It was as if Jesus had just said the worst thing in the world to him. He held the piece of sand in his palm.

"This represents everything I was able to do in my own strength. This, too, I give You, for Your glory and honor and praise." The Lord clutched it in His hands like the beautiful treasure it was. Jesus and he stood there with their arms around each other's shoulders, looking into each other's eyes.

I walked around the tabernacle, realizing that I had been taken up in that moment so much that I had hardly recognized my surroundings. The walls were inlaid with gold and in them were all different colored jewels encrusted into the gold walls. Each jewel was at least the size of my fist. The ceiling had large, trunk-like beams that were embedded within a robin's egg blue sky. The room had large, curved benches with no backs as if people could sit and listen to a speaker there. This was only the outer room. This place was huge!

THE PRINCE OF PEACE

Jesus suddenly stood in front of me. I knew my glimpse was over of the Temple. I asked Him, "What's that smell?"

"Cedar. [14]" He replied. It was already time to go. This was just a little peek.

I looked back at Samuel. Jesus was still standing there with him. Then, I looked out the door and Jesus was standing on the steps. He looked back for me. It was a moment I will never ever forget. I heard the sky erupt with a gentle, but exuberant song. It sounded like the voices of a million women. They sang a love song to the King. "I love you, I love you, I love you..."

But all of this faded into the woodwork, taking a far backseat to His *face* [15]. I walked slowly down the stairs to where He was. He was caught up with me in the moment as well. I looked at His soft, dark eyes. I touched His thick, brown Arab- looking eyebrows. I brushed back His shoulder-length dark hair. We held unto each other's elbows as my left temple touched his left temple.

There was no moment of love in my life like it. The rest of the city became engulfed in a haze around us and even the beautiful song was muffled by the tangible love. We must have stood there like that for a half hour or more, me just taking in His majestic peace.

The moment faded and then I started to continue down the stairs again. He held onto me and I looked back at Him again. The moment started all over again. It was even more love than before and He was even more beautiful. I kissed His shoulder and turned saying, "I could do that forever."

"You will." He said.

THE SILVERSMITH

We walked across the street hand in hand with Pat lagging behind us still taking in the sights. We walked into a small stone building. It was a jewelry shop, filled with silver jewelry. The silversmith stood behind a massive counter covered in glass, protecting the jewelry beneath. Each bracelet was tucked into a royal blue velvet and had a small, white tag with numbers on it. The Lord mused over the selection that seemed identical to me. Pat hummed as she looked at the displays of wind chimes by the door.

Jesus finally made His selection. He chose a thin, silver bracelet. My gold bracelets magically appeared on my arms. I looked at the one on my right arm. It represented a very special gift the Lord created for that arm in particular. The gift of healing. It was my favorite. The Lord took the silver bracelet and placed it with the single gold bracelet. "The silver bracelet represents the purification process. It is why all the basins and bathtubs in the City of God are inlaid with silver. Silver shows purity of spirit."

"Look, Pat," I said holding up my new gift. She held up her two arms with a chuckle. Her sleeves slid down to reveal her arms covered in silver bracelets.

"I've been through this a few times..." she said.

"She's had a lot to walk through, Amy." He whispered. I nodded in understanding.

THE INTERLUDE

For the next two to three days, I could feel a heat around my shins. I saw the Lord bent down beside me, strapping on a kind of soft armor from my knees to my ankles. They were like gray rags, strapped to my legs, girding me up for the next wave of visions[15].

THE GOSPEL OF PEACE

I looked up at Jesus standing in front of me on the street of the city. He was holding a small shell– like a clam. It looked like it was still alive and slightly wet. Inside was a gift for me. "What do you think is inside?" He teased and teased. When I could not take the suspense any longer, He opened it. It exploded with stars which blew directly from the opened shell to the sky above. (To my surprise, the sky was black with night and many stars were already out. There was no moon and definitely no sun. And yet, the whole city was lit up by the radiance of the face of Christ.)

The explosion flew past the sky and my spirit saw beyond the galaxy of stars I was in. It burst from it to fill a void in space and blanketed it with it's starry host. "A new galaxy." He mused. "It is for you. I will name it for you if you wish." The days of creation were over, I thought. I was in astonishment. "Do you like it?" The Lord asked hesitantly.

"It's not that I don't like it, Lord. It's just that..."

"What is it?" He tried to hide a smile.

"If you would look into my heart and give me the gift there..."

I suddenly had a view of Earth as if from space. I saw the continent of Africa. I drew a pentagon in an area towards the eastern part of Africa. The point of the pentagon pointed to the east. I continued with a heavenly knowledge, "This area of the world is full of pain. I feel it every day. There women and children have been raped. They are without food. They are tortured daily by the sun and the guerillas around them. I am broken hearted for them and wish to gather them up in my arms. Give them peace as a gift to me."

He turned towards me. We were back on the street again. "Only My bride would ask for something like that... I will do this for you, My love." I saw in the spirit a group of people, who felt like Christians in the spirit. They built a well there inside the area of the pentagon I drew. When the water burst out, they were all dancing and singing. I sighed in relief.

I looked back at Him. He touched my long wavy hair. "The King is held captive by your tresses." He said.

"What significance does hair have, Lord?" Immediately I saw a vision of a Lion and a lioness walking, I could see the Lion's mane rippling with the wind.

"Hair represents My glory. I am held captive by My glory I have put on you."

THE GIFT STORE

We walked towards another white building. Inside was filled with rectangular boxes all the same size, like shoe boxes, piled in neat rows along the walls. Each was wrapped differently. "Pick one out for Pat," He said excitedly. I felt like I was playing Santa as Pat grabbed the emerald box I selected for her. She opened it.

"It's a house!" She yelled. My eyes got huge. She needed a house badly. I looked back at the pile. My faith soar. These are not just gifts of the Spirit in here! These were things we had prayed for. These boxes were for the remnant. God was giving them out. I selected a pink box on my left. In it contained a large, silver and gold bangle, much like the ones I had on my arms. This one was bigger however and I wondered how I was going to keep it on my arm. The Lord took it and showed me that it was actually two bangles that interlocked together. He undid them and held them out.

"They are anklets," He informed me as I slipped them over my shoes. "They are for you to walk in righteousness."

Although it was a stupid question, I still asked, "What is righteousness?"

"Doing what is right."

In the dirt floor beside me was a large hole. The Lord reached into it and pulled out a fat, white rat the size of a cat. He held it facing me under it's arms. I drew back. "Catch for me the little foxes, Amy. The little foxes that ruin our vineyards." He them reached in and brought up another rat identical to the other. They were going to start a family and reproduce! They were the enemy, seeking to destroy what God had prepared for His people. Two angels appeared at the doorway with two cages. He put the rats in it and they took them away.

We walked out to the street. Appearing all over our bodies was the jewelry that had been given to us during our stay in the city. We had our bangles on, clanging against each other as we moved. I had on my two beautiful pink stones of intercession. Pat had on her ruby earrings of prophecy and her ring of intercession. She carried in one hand a velvet box containing her earrings of evangelism. Under her other arm was tucked the box with her "house" in it. We trotted along merrily. I commented to the Lord as He touched the gem between my eyes lovingly. "We need a cart for all the stuff you've given us here!"

"No, you need something much bigger than that," He mused, "You need your faith to bring it all back home in."

The Lord started walking backwards in front of us. I tried to warn Him about the black light posts behind Him, but it was too late. Much to my surprise, however, He walked right through them. And as we followed, we also walked through them. He told us with authority, "Every door that is shut will be open to you. I have to go first, however."

THE MUSIC STORE

We walked toward another simple building. It was a music store. But it did not hold musical instruments or sheet music. It was actual music. I could see it in the air being played as it was written on bars of music. It was beautifully being entwined and played at the same time, but sounded beautiful- as if it was all in the same key. A bar of music flew into my open mouth and went straight down to my belly. When it flew out, a song came out that I could not stop if I had tried. I sang triumphantly:

"You are my King!
You are the Mighty One!
You are the Majestic One!
You are the only true God!"

He interrupted me, as I sang one revelation of who He was after another, with a song all His own. His voice was more beautiful than any man's on Earth. **He** sang,

"I AM YOURS!
I AM YOURS!

49

I AM YOURS!"

I met my voice with Him and sang, "I am Yours [17]!" with Him. I was totally intoxicated with the fact that the King of Kings, the Maker of the universe, the God of all gods was telling me that He is mine. How could I contain my tears?

"I am the conductor, Amy. I am the conductor of all your affairs here and on Earth." We walked out. Pat stayed behind in the music store for hours as we went outside to the street.

CHAPTER 5

THE FATHER OF LIGHTS

O n the street, a rainbow appeared and zoomed straight into me from some source. It started with the purple color around my forehead and then changed colors all the way down to my torso to display a yellow color. Each bar of color was going into a different part of my body vertically. Each part of the Body was anointed differently [18].

I looked up and as far as I could see was the **throne**- with the Father Himself sitting upon it. I was no bigger than His baby toe. He was awesome! This is how I had always thought of Him, as too big and too awesome to approach. I had always clung to Jesus because He seemed so much more approachable, but my heart craved out for my Father.

He miniaturized Himself instantly to my size near His gigantic feet. I felt more at ease. He was still beautiful and awesome. I hesitated. But my longing grew too deep as I caught a glimpse of Him smiling, His face surrounded with a fog. I ran to Him, still a little afraid. I became a four year old little girl with pig tails again. I bounced onto His lap. He chuckled. His beautiful, soft robe, started at His waist. His muscle mass was thick. I smelled the skin on His shoulder. It smelled like the beach, salty and wonderful. "He has been hovering over the waters of the deep," Jesus said.

"Can I kiss Your face?" I asked in my little voice.

"Of course you can!" He said like a proud Grandfather. He continued gently, "Most people are too scared and intimidated by Me to kiss My face, but I long for the affection." I kissed His face all over as He laughed heartily. I loved that He was laughing. I could hear Jesus laughing, too. I started to get down and then "surprised" Him again with more little kisses like a little child would. I finally got down and started walking back to Jesus. I went back to my earthly age of 28, again.

I put my arms around the Lord to thank Him for that moment with the Father. The Father and His throne vanished and it was just the two of us again. "Thank you," I whispered. He held me close and then pointed to the sky. I still couldn't get over that it was actually night. It seemed like it was the middle of the day. The stars winked at me as He "drew" in the air with His pointer finger. To my amazement, the stars started moving and getting in line with what He was drawing with them. They finally displayed the cursive letters for the word, "Love."

"I will write what I have to in the night sky to my Bride," He said. He never stopped surprising me.

THE MAP

Standing on the street again, He stood in front of me with a large paper, scrolled up. "This is a treasure map, Amy."

"How do I read this, Lord?" I could not see any map on it as He unrolled it before me. It seemed to be old and faded. Then, suddenly, on the left side of the paper, a hologram of a cave appeared as if it was the starting point. Pat came out of the music store by this time, full of songs, and stood beside me as the Lord vanished. *He'll never leave me or forsake me*, I reminded myself. I took a deep breath and looked to the left. On a small hill above the music store was a cave that looked identical to the map. *He sure does simplify things*, I thought to myself.

We entered the dark cave. The moment we stepped in, we sunk to our chest in black ink-like fluid. *This has got to be wrong. This must be just me. This can't be from the Lord*, I panicked. It was almost completely black in the cave, even though there was an opening. It seemed as though darkness was trapped inside it. "Your fear of darkness," I felt the Holy Spirit say.

I felt around for some sort of opening, after all, this was a *starting* place, it must lead to somewhere. Directly in front of me, under the fluid, was a round passage way. I held my breath and started in it. My body barely fit through it and I was afraid I would drown. "Your fear of enclosed space and drowning," I felt the Holy Spirit say.

I broke through the skin of the fluid and stepped into the abyss. I took a deep breath in as I made my way into some sort of clearing. I was in space! I started falling very quickly down, down, down. "Your fear of falling," I felt the Holy Spirit say.

I looked down and saw I was in a ravine on Earth and was almost going to hit when a man grabbed me from a ledge. His face was fierce and he held me by my throat over the cliff. He then put a gun to my head and pulled the trigger. It did not go off! "Your fear of man," I felt the Holy Spirit say.

Then, I saw a man sitting on a throne just like the Father. But this man was not my God. I had died and was standing before a different religion's god. "Your fear of making the wrong choice in Me," I felt the Holy Spirit say. I was ashamed.

Then, all went dark. Dark enough to go crazy. And I was alone. "Your fear of losing Me," I felt the Holy Spirit say. This was the deepest one. The one that hurts when brought to light.

THE HEART

I opened my eyes. Pat, who I had not seen since the cave, was standing next to me. The Lord was standing in front of me. The map was open and the middle part of it came to life with a real heart, beating in midair over it. *Boom, boom. Boom, boom.* "This is My heart," The Lord said, the gravity of which sinking down inside us. *Boom, boom. Boom, boom.* The heartbeat of Heaven before us.

My own skin became transparent and I could see my own heart inside me beating. It had gold threads twisting through it still from the band that had sunk into me. It was turning it silently into almost solid gold. When the Lord reached in to grab hold of it, it finished it's work just in time to release a solid gold heart. He held it in His hand, beating. "You thought I was renewing your heart with this gold, but I was just making it valuable enough to trade for this." He pointed to His own heart, still beating on the map.

His heart was transplanted into me by Him. I felt myself being lifted up. Jesus stood in front of me in midair and sort of danced in a circle. He went *through* me at the opposite point of the circle He was making– instead of around me. That moment felt strange, like I was in Him and He in Me.

Then, I could feel His heart start to beat in me. I knew in that moment the heart of Jesus. It was simply this– unbelievable surrender to the Father's will. He did not take a breath unless the Father willed Him to. Every second. Every moment. Nothing of His own. Everything for the Father. "Let them be in Me as I am in You.[19]"

I closed my eyes. He took me through the cave of fears again in lightning speed. I held onto Him as if He was apart of me now. Siamese twins. There was no fear this time in anything I experienced. No fear in the cave, the tunnel, space, the man, the gun, the god, not even a hint of feeling like I was ever, ever going to lose Him. It was all gone [20].

CHAPTER 6

PSALM 46

The Lord pulled me close to Him. Suddenly, a wind with so much humidity and moisture in it that it felt like a river, blew like a hurricane through the streets of the city. Jesus and I bursts into laughter– He more so than I. Pat collapsed on the street, laughing her heart out. As the river of wind blew through the city, I could hear laughter coming from inside the buildings [21] .

A staircase appeared in front of us. Standing at the foot of it, it looked like a ladder [22]. The stairs had no rails and they were made out of some kind of spiritual material that resembled glass– but they moved slightly. The wind let up enough just around us to climb up the stairs, the Lord and I, hand in hand. We climbed and climbed. A long gown with a train appeared on me. It was a beautiful, red velvet.

At long last, we arrived in the small opening as angels on either sides helped us up into the heavenly atmosphere. We stood there as Jesus motioned for me to look in front of us. It took a few seconds for my eyes to adjust to the brightness. On both sides of us were tangles upon tangles of gorgeous, pink flowers. They looked like a cross breed between a rose and a camellia. They moved with life. They bent backwards and made paths for us as we walked. They came up to me like an animal. I smelled the sweet fragrance.

Finally, I could see straight ahead of us. A very narrow, gold building with a small, gold staircase that went up to it was just beyond us. We climbed the few steps. The Lord put His hand on the small of my back and said, "Brace yourself." The door opened and praise and worship blew out. It would have knocked me flat on my back and maybe off the stairs if the Lord had not braced me so.

We entered the building. It was an unbelievably long, narrow building that seemed to go on forever. There was stadium seating on both sides of a long aisle that went straight through the building. Saints were sitting and standing all through the bleachers, worshiping. The music was beautiful and it actually was able at times to lift us off of our feet.

"Why is this aisle here, Lord? Is it for You to walk through?"

"No, it is for the River!" He cried out as water poured through the open front door. It lifted us off of our feet and carried us through the building. I noticed that there were a few books around us, floating on the River, as we surfed the Wave. It finally started receding. We started walking back through where it had come in. On both sides of the aisle, every single person was laying or crouched down, unable to speak. They had been waiting for it!

THE OCEAN

We walked out and turned left. The pink flowers looked at us and started making a path for us. Not far down the path, I stepped innocently, seeing and thinking that I was just taking another step onto the road, when it became an ocean. All around us was ocean. There was lightning hitting all around us. The clouds poured in like a horrific storm was approaching. I held on tight to the hand of the Lord. The waves picked up and down like moving hills. We walked on the water as we talked.

"What is this place, Lord?"

"It is My heart. I am heartbroken." He sighed, single tears escaping His eyes. I listened, unable to speak. "My Body does not love Me as they should. They only love Me because I heal them." He paused, looking away from me. "They only love Me because of what I sacrificed for them."

He looked towards me with anger in His voice, "Imagine how you would feel if I only loved you because of what you sacrificed for Me." I started to cry, too. We sat down on the waves as if it was a rug.

"There's only so much you can do, Lord. You have given men free will..." He stared into the atmosphere, not answering me. Up and down, the waves got worse. I then had an idea. "Maybe there is something the Holy Spirit can do!" He looked at me as if He was waiting for me to figure out the answer.

"I will go ask Him." He said, getting up, taking my hand and walking out of the storm room.

Before we left, I asked the question I did not want to ask.. "Do I love You as I should?"

"You are starting to," He said with a small smile.

"Just wanted to know I was on the right path."

"You are definitely on the right path," He said. We put our feet on the path and everything went back as it was before. The flowers hurried out of our way as Jesus walked with a mission down the road. We turned left, directly beyond the direction we came in.

THE PARTNERSHIP

There was another, huge building. We went up the white stairs and stopped. He looked at me before the door opened. "Do not be overwhelmed by this." Easy for Him to say! I was so overwhelmed by what I had already seen. I felt my flesh start to moan from the magnitude of it all and considered going back to it on Earth. I thought of returning to Earth. But the Lord caught me back by His beautiful face and I could not leave.

The doors opened. A huge ballroom like the one I had been with Him after the honey tree was before me. Maybe it was even the same one and I was seeing it clearly and brightly now. Huge, beautiful pink and white marble tiles spread all over the floor and people and angels were everywhere except for a large path they made in the middle [24].

The throne of God with the Father on it was directly in front of me. "Amy," the Father said. I honestly did not recognize my own name, I was in such awe. Jesus touched me on the elbow.

I mouthed the word, "Daddy," as I gazed at Him. I felt like I had been separated from Him for years, as if He had come home from a war. I ran to Him and flew into His lap, not caring one iota about what anyone else thought. I hugged His neck and cried. He did, too.

"I want to thank you, Amy," He said slowly and gently. "You comforted Me while J'oshua was on the cross." I couldn't believe He was saying it to me. Did He *really* see me then? Tears dripped from both our faces. I looked over to see Jesus at the foot of the stairs to the throne, kneeling in intercession.

I looked back to the Father, who I still could not see clearly, and asked the same thing I knew Jesus was asking. "Father, send Your Holy Spirit to Earth. Help them to love Your Son as they should." He nodded.

Into the throne room came the Holy Spirit who looked like a gigantic, ghost-like piece of material. He hovered and swam, turning and twisting over our heads around Jesus and the throne of the Father. He duplicated Himself and flew down to the planet Earth far below us, but visible from a window in the Spirit near the throne. He blanketed and caressed the planet and stayed there.

I walked down towards Jesus, who was now standing. He took my hand. "You're ready," He said and nodded to the Father. A huge zipper appeared in front of us and Jesus pulled it open. Black space was in it and we stepped in, holding tightly to each other.

We went down, down, down, back to Earth. I went through the roof of my house and finally, stood with the Lord in my living room. I glanced over to see my body, laying on the couch, still in my white bath robe. I opened my eyes back in my body at home.

THE SHEEP

An hour later, I arrived back at the park bench in the City of God. The bench was still turned around, facing the East. Jesus and Pat were sitting there. Jesus stood up very quickly when He saw me like a school boy with a crush on me. It looked suddenly like it was going to rain, as the wind blew through His hair. Then, the weather returned to it's cheery self just as quickly.

I smiled at the two of them. He offered me the place He had been sitting. He seemed like He needed to talk to me badly. He knelt down in front of me, which I hated because I always wanted Him far above me. He took my two hands in His and very seriously said, "I need to ask you a question, Amy." I nodded for Him to continue. He looked at Pat for a reassuring glance and said to me, "Feed my sheep [25]." It was a proposal like none other.

Immediately, sheep appeared from behind Him. There were several large sheep there. One had a tiny, little lamb. The lamb looked out from under the big sheep's rear end. The big sheep stated, *"baaaa,"* in protest. He was grumpy. I knelt down and started playing with them. Each had a distinct personality that seemed human. They were so adorable.

"What will I feed them?" I asked. Immediately, a leather satchel appeared around me. It was the one I had worn on my way in the city the first day. I had caught the diamonds in it! Inside were no diamonds. There was only sheep-food pellets. I smiled and started handing them out. The sheep crowded around me, trying to get to my hands filled with food. They bit and tore at my clothes of blue and gray. (I was wearing robes of some kind.) I laughed with great patience, trying to get to all of them.

The Lord seemed pleased as He stood up, motioning ahead of us. The park where our tents had been was a beautiful hillside, warm and green. He strolled with me, leaving Pat on the bench, soaking up the warmth of the day. The sheep trotted merrily behind us as we lead them to a beautiful, hilly clearing with a little stream below. I lay back on the hill, Jesus standing near me. I put my hands behind my head and watched the sheep graze.

"Am I going to meet David here?" I asked in excited anticipation. Only the Lord had known that my secret desire since arrival was to run into him, my favorite servant of the Lord.

"I'm looking at him," The Lord said looking straight at me. What? He handed me a small harp. "This is a time of preparation. This is the thing kings are made of. David was chosen to be the shepherd because he was the youngest. Jesse never thought he would add up to anything. But something happened in the lonesomeness of days and nights being out here. He fell in love with Me. He looked up to these same stars and loved me.

"You have thought that I hid you away like this because you were not worth enough to Me to place you in a ministry. Don't you remember how I anointed you with the same oil I anointed David king with?"

(I recalled what He talked about with clarity. I had been at a prayer service at my church. The Lord ushered me out and told me to go to a back room. There He appeared before me, a huge, gold lamp of oil in His hands. He spoke these words over me, "This is the same oil I used to anoint David king." He poured it over me, tangibly feeling the warm oil drip all over me.)

The grass on the hill moved with the wind of His words. *"You* are my David for this generation. I will place you on a hill that no wind can remove you from."

I stood up, my legs wobbly from laying there so long. He led me down to the little brook. A lamb was drinking there and he looked at us puzzled as we drank in the sugary water. Jesus stuck His whole head in, coming up, shaking His hair like a mane. He looked at me with His hair dripping on His shoulders. No one is more beautiful. I sighed. "Why did you do that?" I asked, thinking there was a great revelation in it.

"I was hot." He said as I laughed. "I *am* alive, you know [26]." At that moment, it became very real to me. He is alive! Not just a spirit roaming around. He has a body!

CHAPTER 7

THE WALK

"You know that huge skyscraper building I saw when I first arrived?" I changed the subject.

"The administration building?"

"Yea!" I said thinking it cool that He confirmed that it was what I thought. "Can we go there now?"

"I don't see why not," He said, surprising me. He held out His hand for me to take and we walked back towards the park bench. Pat was sitting there, her eyes closed, rocking. She rubbed her face. Jesus took her right hand from her face and squeezed it. She did not open her eyes or stop a moment, never missing a beat, as if it never happened. She did not even know we walked passed her. She was in intercession for someone.

As we walked, Jesus taught. "You are trying to forgive people who have hurt you by making sense of what happened. You are trying to form excuses for them. You are trying to say to yourself that you have done worse, so you have to forgive them. But that doesn't work does it? It just keeps coming back.

"What you have to do, Amy, and what you must teach people who have been hurt very badly to do is to get in My presence and receive a dose of love for that person that is undescribable. That way, when they come at you with a cat of nine tales, smacking your face, you can look up at them with My eyes and say, 'Please, do that again. Do whatever you want. I love you no matter what.'"

We walked down the street. I looked up towards the window of the bath house, feeling a rain of diamonds come down again. I held on tight to the hand of the Lord.

THE ADMINISTRATION BUILDING

We turned right at the gate and entered the very small, but very tall, building. It was a crystal building. Inside, it was like a small hotel lobby, bustling and busy. The woman at the front desk glanced up while on the phone and quickly ended her conversation to greet us. A bell boy buzzed by. "Amy is ready to go on the elevator." Within the second, the girl was on the phone. Immediately, a crystal elevator appeared twenty feet or so in front of us. It *dinged* as it opened it's doors to let us in.

The door closed behind us and we were silently on our way. I could see each floor as it flew passed us. Some were going so fast, I was having a hard time processing what I was seeing. Each floor was a level in my life. This elevator was my transportation through my life! I was going to see it all again- very quickly.

The first scene I recognized was when I was about three years old. I just couldn't seem to grow hair on my head. My mother had told me that my Daddy had always wanted a little girl with two little pony tails. I was going to be that little girl! I was determined. So, I dragged my little stool in front of my mother and had her squeeze and pull my little hairs so tightly it hurt. She put two little clips in my hair with tiny shoots of hair peaking though. When my Daddy came home, I ran to him screaming, "Look, Daddy! Pigtails!" He was so happy.

The elevator went fast. I caught another scene. My first date with my first real boyfriend. My linen dress, tan skin. My eighteenth birthday. I smiled as he stood up when he saw me. He was so unbelievably handsome. I smiled over at Jesus on the other side of the elevator, holding onto the rails. He smiled back at me, knowingly.

THE NOW

The elevator went even faster. I caught another scene of me just days ago in Heaven, seeing the Father on the throne. Then, the elevator caught up to us and stopped. It *dinged.* "Where are we?" I asked.

"We are in the now," Jesus replied as the doors swung open. I looked out. I could not see even a hint of the administration building we were suppose to be in. I clung to the railing on the opposite side of the elevator in fear. We were in midair! About a hundred stories down was green grass. I could see no sign of the city. Just beautiful, green country side. "It's time to step out! He said.

Time to step out? Time to step out? Had He totally lost it? There was no way.

"We are in the present. You must step out of the elevator."

I shook my head in defiance. He stood there, motionless. My tight grip on the bar along the elevator grew sweaty. I knew what I had to do. I had walked on waves before, after all. But not without His hand. Always with His hand. I had an idea. "Not without You, Lord. You have to hold onto me the whole time." I threw myself at Him and wrapped my arms around His waist. We stepped out of the elevator. We stood in midair. I opened my eyes. I took His hand in another moment of faith and let Him breathe a little.

"You must let go of me and stand here on your own," He informed me.

No and uh-uh.

In front of us, standing also in midair, appeared a huge number of people. Maybe about ten thousand or more. In the front were people dear to me that had either accepted Christ through me or were making plans to. Behind them, were people from all different races. People I had never seen before. Jesus spoke, "These are all people who will love Me because You stepped out. You must let go." I clung harder.

We flew up above the crowd and stood in the middle of them. Their heads were under our feet. "If I let go now," I reasoned, "I could fall and I would take a lot of people down with me." I saw how I could fall right into a lot of them. Why did God have to make this even harder?

In a moment of not thinking, I let go. Jesus immediately vanished. I did not move a muscle. I just stood there in midair, above all those people. *I was not falling.* I stood there for about a minute.

I closed my eyes and opened them again. I had passed the test. My fear of falling from a position of authority– gone. I was standing at the bus station in the City, Jesus in front of me. "You must go back now," He said. I opened my eyes, back home in my bedroom.

I closed them again, "No!"

I saw Him again. He repeated again, "You must go back now." And I did.

CHAPTER 8

For the next few days, I heard Him whispering again and again, "I don't *want* to leave you, I don't *want* to leave you..." Not only was He not going to leave me, He never wants to.

The whispers became more real and more clear as my spirit embodied on the bus station platform days later. Holding onto His elbows, and He mine, His face became visible again in the beautiful city. We walked back towards the park. The green hills were still lush and filled with little sheep. The hills rolled in beauty, but I found myself wanting to go on and explore other things– not to linger in the same spot I had been. The sheep bit at our clothes as we stood laughing in the green fields, our arms around each other.

THE HERO

My eyes caught a glimpse of a bright glitter on a far hill. It was a small, gold harp, shining in the sunlight. Someone was holding it. *David!* Not even giving myself a chance to scream his name like a star-struck fan, I ran up and down the hills until I got to him. The Lord strolled along slowly, it seemed, but got to David at the same time as me somehow. David stood up when he saw me and grinned widely. We clasped arms. "Amy, my sister!" He beamed.

"My big brother!" I gushed happily. His small, gold crown was almost covered by large, black curls all over his head. He was maybe an inch shorter than I and seemed to be about sixteen or seventeen. He had laid his harp down on the grass when I approached. He was tan and his face was slightly wrinkled around the eyes. He smiled so brightly that I could hardly take it. *And yet, nothing but a shepherd,* I thought in unbelief of what God had done.

We would have looked like we were ignoring the Lord standing behind me, but we were not. Our hearts were steadfast focused on Him and what He wanted to do with this moment. He was overseeing us with great joy, united. David immediately began giving me the information that I desperately needed. We giggled and hugged each other, sweaty from the heat of the day.

"Look beyond those hills over there." He pointed as far as I could see. "There will be times in the cave, but do not worry about those times because my Lord will be there with you as He was with me. They will be wonderful times as long as He is there. And He will be. There will be times of caves, but there will also be times of castles. Be wary that your weaknesses do not overwhelm (or take over) you there [in the castle]. You have an advantage over me. You have Him in the fullness. He will help you overcome your weaknesses. Do not worry [27]."

He continued as the words sunk deep within my spirit, "Remember, the battle is the Lord's. You *have* to *ask* Him how to win it each time [28]. Do not use a previous method to win a different battle. It will not work. And, your enemy will start to know you. Always ask Him."

He kissed the palm of my hand and put it on his heart. "Although, I was a king in a castle, I asked the Lord if I could go back to the shepherd's hill and stay there for eternity with Him. It is the most glorious time. Keep your eye on the sheep, though. Make sure that you raise your children to be able to take over for you and finish what you can not, if the need arises." With that, he handed me jewelry. I closed my hand quickly, catching a glimpse of gold and sapphires.

I thought maybe it was another bracelet. I marveled at his face and mannerisms. So much like Jesus'! I couldn't believe it. Steven had said that everyone had His mannerisms up here- but this was just too much.

I turned and walked away with Jesus, back through the hills. "He's so much like You, Lord."

"That is why I chose him," Jesus said quietly.

ANOTHER TREE, ANOTHER STORM

We left David and walked towards our left so far that we couldn't even see the bench. In fact, we couldn't see the city anymore. Wind picked up and great clouds started to form in the sunless sky. It grew a little darker than usual. A huge tree appeared in front of us. It's trunk was huge. It's limbs started about ten feet from the base and were lush with little, green leaves. We ran towards it. Although this probably would not have been a good idea on Earth, it seemed that the laws of nature were slightly different here. This was shelter from the storm.

Underneath it, we caught our breaths. The rain poured down immediately, but not a drop went through the thick ceiling of leaves above us. We sat down together, side by side. Jesus had a blue, white, gold, and silver Jewish prayer shawl draped around Him that was huge. He covered His own head and mine with it. I played with the tassels on the end.

(The *wings* of the prayer shawl.) They seemed dry, but when I twisted them in my fingers, they left an oily residue [29].

We sat like that for it seemed hours. I watched as the rain formed tiny little streams on the ground that were now leaking a little into our area. The lightning began hitting like a hammer around us. It got darker. "What's in your hand, woman?" He asked almost forcefully. I opened my hand that was still clasped with David's gift. Three smooth stones! Where were the jewels?

"You will need weapons out here," He said, reminding me of how David fought off a lion from his flock.

I was suddenly surprised to make out a dark image of a person about fifty yards from us. It was a woman, a shadow in the distance. I stood up, His shawl sliding off my head. He stood up as I raced to the person, lightning hitting all around her. I grabbed her wet hand and practically flung her into the shelter of the tree.

Next, a man's large hand petrified me as it appeared on my shoulder. I spun around and pulled that man in as well. I was getting soaked and cold. Another person appeared, another. I pushed and pulled them into safety. I was muddy. There must have been about forty or more of them. I coughed from the workout, my body not in shape enough to keep up. The lightning stopped.

The Lord took one step out of the tree's shelter, His prayer shawl still hanging from His head. He looked tall. He stretched out His arm to me. *I'm finished.* And there He was. The people were packed in and I didn't even know if there was room for me anymore. I don't know how else to say it, but there was great pride for me in His eyes. I held onto His hands as we floated like a balloon straight up. The storm stopped and I dried off instantly [30].

We both closed our eyes, our faces upwards. Warmth was all around us. He had a leather satchel around His waist like the one I fed the sheep from. Inside looked like gold dust! He reached into it and gave me a handful as He took His own. In fact, they were very, very tiny gold seeds. We began tossing them out, sowing the ground beneath us, including the people still under the tree.

"I need you in this final hour," He said.

The people under the tree turned into huge, golden stems that went straight up and twisted through the ceiling of leaves. As if someone waved their magic wand, they each vanished with a flurry of gold dust. It was as if they were spiders, invisibly gliding on their spinners in the wind– each searching and finding their destiny. I was amazed at this rebirth [31].

We went down an invisible staircase from the air above the tree to the ground. Everything seemed so peaceful without the people there anymore. Underneath the tree again, the day started feeling sleepy. The tree sprouted a gorgeous extension of thin, satin ribbons. They grew from the farthest points of the tree limbs and cascaded down like my willow did. Each ribbon was a different color and moved gently with the wind [32].

I gasped quietly. The Lord had been watching this display in admiration as well. He finally turned to me. His shoulders took up so much space under the tree that I almost had to step back as He turned. He was an awesome figure.

He put one of His hands about six inches in the air from my waist on the left, and the other in the same fashion on my right. Then, He forcefully moved His hands outward, then inward in the air. When His hands returned to their original position, I heard a large clap, like lightning. I looked down, and I was wearing a beautiful white gown with no sleeves [33]. On the back, where my neck was were rainbow ribbons to match the tree. The ribbons fell down my back and onto the ground like a train. My hair was pulled back as well.

THE WATERFALL

He led me by the hand, though the curtain of ribbons. The ribbons petted me from head to ankle as I walked. Outside of the tree, it was very bright. We walked a few steps and a massive waterfall appeared. It must have been about ten to fifteen stories high, with only a little pool of water beneath about fifty by fifty feet.

He seemed giddy and danced with me there. I was glad no one else was around. We stopped and He hugged me, His huge arms almost dwarfing my small frame. He kissed the back of my hair and in reckless emotion whispered, "I want to marry you." It was almost as if He wasn't suppose to say that, like something was holding Him back, but He just couldn't resist any longer.

My head spun with the word, "marry". In an instant, every meaning was brought up like my mind was a computer dictionary: "to draw near", "to make a covenant", "to become one with." And somehow I knew exactly what He meant. *How very interesting*, I thought. In our small view point, this moment could be taken so very fleshly, but *here*, it seemed so much different. It felt like the promise and the commitment above all commitments. It felt like an inheritance of indescribable proportions. It felt like a spiritual union of wills.

He looked over to the waterfall, not looking at me. He motioned for me to step in, His eyes towards the ground. I put my foot in, with my purple satin shoe on. It was cool water. I put the other foot in, proud of myself for being brave enough to go in to my ankles.

The Lord looked at me, smiled, and threw Himself in on His right side. He came up sopping wet, laughing. He hugged me teasingly, getting me soaked on the front of my dress. He laughed heartily. I looked at the waterfall, thinking how very nice it would be... and since I was already wet....[34]

The water got to about my bellybutton when I finally reached the falls. It showered down on my hair. It did not feel like water, though, it felt like wind. Each droplet felt like a microscopic fish was boring into my pores and going into my flesh. It didn't feel bad, though, just strange. I remembered the verse, "The river of God is teaming with life...[35]"

The song "Fairest Lord Jesus [36]" was being sung all around me and in me. Each word dripped into me like the little fish. I absorbed every word. I walked out of the water, dry as a bone. I went back over to the Lord who was beaming and drying off quickly as well. I was still ankle deep in the water.

A huge, bright-red fish appeared. It looked like a koi as big as a cat. It came up to me like it wanted to be touched. "Remember the time I had all those fish come up to you, just because you asked Me to?"

(I remembered the event well. The previous summer I had stayed in a hotel where there was a waterfall and pond in the lobby- huge and beautiful. A large koi came up towards me. I had asked the Lord to bring all the koi up to me. Within just two or three seconds, every koi had rushed from all over the pond to where I was standing. I had reasoned that it was just because they thought I had food. But there were many people around the waters edge then....)

"These fish do not want to be fed, and they still come up to you," He continued, leaning over to gently grasp the red fish. The fish willing was picked up and put into a silver basket shaped like a heart that appeared from nowhere. The Lord carried it in one hand, the fish lightly flopping inside of it. Even though I knew I was not on Earth, I still had great compassion for the fish and asked the Lord to put it back. He smiled at me, knowing that He was not hurting the fish and took the fish out of the basket and faced it to me in the air. "Take the ring out of it's mouth." I reached into the fish's mouth and brought out a diamond ring [37].

"Wash it off before you put it on me!" I teased the Lord. He let the fish go and rinsed the ring off in the water. He put it on my finger and with it came a revelation: Out of His hands and creation will come everything I will need for the demands of the World. He provided the disciples taxes like this. And now, I would need something of great value to give to the world as well.

THE MANLY BRIDE

We turned towards the direction we had originally come and started walking in the warmth of the day. Sheep started appearing all around us and I realized that the waterfall was actually pouring not only into the little pool, but it branched out to the little brook I had seen on the hillside. We followed the stream back. The waterfall was its source!

Then, I saw David again! He stood up when he saw me. I thought I would never see him again. We embraced immediately. "I am so happy to see you!" I beamed.

"And I, you!" He seemed a little bit more serious than before.

"I will not let you go until you bless me this time!" I heard myself demanding. This was not like me.

He had me kneel in front of him, he placed his hands on my head. "May you become nothing. May you become as dust. May your name disappear from the Earth. And may He be your music." This was not the blessing I was expecting. But I felt my body absorb every word to be truth. *I must become less, so He can become more* [38]. I couldn't get back up. In fact, I couldn't move at all. But I could see and knew everything happening around me.

David walked away from me and toward the Lord who was watching at a safe distance. He embraced His arms, each holding onto the other's elbows. "This is what you are to me, my Lord." David wept openly. "You are my song!" They embraced, the two manliest men in the word, held onto each other crying. It reminded me of my moments of love with the Master. It didn't seem to be any different for him than me.

Then David, tears still dripping from His face, knelt down to the Lord's feet and kissed the middle toe on His left foot. *"You* are the King!" David cried out, trying to rip off his own crown. The Lord stopped him, David's crown never having the chance to leave his head.

"I gave that to you. You are a king as well." Jesus spoke reassuringly, but it did not make any difference. David did not agree with the final decision.

David walked back to me, helping me up. "Don't forget what I taught you."

"Never." I held onto his hand, even as the Lord turned me and started walking me away. We finally lost grasp of each other.

"You two act as if you will never see each other again," Jesus said.

CHAPTER 9

THE LILY OF THE VALLEY

We walked through the park and back onto the front street of town. The city was filled with people bustling around. It was the first time I had actually seen people in the streets. The city was always so very quiet. Now it was alive. People were all over, getting ready for suppertime. There were carts with food and carts with flowers. Everyone was joyous and excited about what the evening would bring.

I walked over to a cart filled with flowers. Next to it, was another cart filled with fresh baked bread. A small man with only one or two hairs on his head was picking out a loaf next to me. I caught his eye. I noticed him watching me, so, normally I would not, but here- here I started up a conversation. "It just occurred to me that I have no money with me," I put my hand in my pocket of my traveling skirt. I had changed back to the wardrobe that I wore days ago when I arrived at the bus station. *When had I done that?* I wondered.

The man laughed a little and said, "You don't understand. You don't need money here. Everything has already been bought and paid for, you just take what you need." I looked up, searching for the Lord who had left my side for the first time in a long time. He was chatting casually with a lady by a door about twenty feet away from me.

"I *have* to pay something for these," I mused, looking at the small bouquet of fragrant lily of the valley. The man nodded in astonishment. The jewelry was all gone from me, as if someone had put it all away before changing me into the ordinary clothes. I remembered the beautiful mother of pearl barrettes in my hair. I thought about just taking one out, but on close inspection of the gorgeous bouquet, I decided to take out both. My hair cascaded into my face as I tucked the two barrettes in where the flowers had been in the cart. "I *must* pay something for a gift for *Him* [39]."

I tucked my hair behind my ear as the Lord came towards me. "For you..." I said, meekly, not knowing if such a man would even except flowers. He took them right away, then looked at me, brushing my hair back with His hand. He looked back at His bouquet, took a dainty, white flower out and twisted it with His two fingers. He then somehow fashioned it into a barrette and wove it into my hair. He did the same with the other side.

"Beautiful," He said.

Lost in our display, the man next to me, cleared his throat. I turned around and looked at him, almost a foot above his head. "I would like to invite you over for dinner," He said to me. "My name is Ezekiel."

"When is dinner!?" I sang out, eagerly. But secretly, I hoped it would be at least a few hours. Ezekiel was one figure in the Bible that I knew little about.

EZEKIEL

"Dinner is now," He astonished me. *Now?* He tucked the loaf under his arm and led us down the path and turned left, the opposite direction of the tabernacle, but not too far away. A small home with one window in front. I had seen this house from the hillside on my arrival to the city. It was a beautiful crystal. When it caught the light of the Lord, it rainbowed out in a sea of beautiful colors. The roof was also crystal, but was covered by a few twigs to shield some of it's beauty. Inside, the walls looked white- washed and stone.

A woman with red, curly hair was cooking at a fireplace. I couldn't tell where the chimney went up and out because almost directly above the fireplace were set-in bunk beds that had been built into the wall. Everything was cozy and simple. The only pieces of furniture in the room were a naked wood table and four chairs. The woman was hard at work, stirring the meat in the pot. She touched the Lord's shoulder as she walked passed Him like He was a dear Son or Father. He smiled at her, wrinkling His eyes. She politely greeted me and set off to work filling small plates with food.

It was like a pot roast. She served the Lord first, who smelled it and gave His plate to me. I tasted a bite before He even *got* another plate and everyone was served. I didn't realize how very hungry I was. We had milk as well, but it was not very cold, which I was not use to. It had a little hair in it and was thicker than any milk I had ever had. I got over it quickly because of my hunger.

We ate in silence, me scarfing down mouth fulls undaintily. I asked the Lord in my mind as to not to offend, "Why is Ezekiel in such a tiny dwelling?" After I asked the question, the room expanded to a huge ballroom with gold pillars and angels painted on the ceiling. We were sitting on gold chairs in the middle of a ballroom, each dressed in fine clothes. I was seeing it as it really was. Then it went back to the original surroundings just as quickly.

"Because it is what he is comfortable with." The Lord returned the inquiry inside my head.

How very interesting that He actually lives in a palace, and yet chooses to live in a small place to feel cozy, I thought.

A song filled the room gently, like someone turning up beautiful music very slowly. I looked up with my mouth full. Ezekiel and the woman were singing, their hands folded and their faces upward with their eyes closed. The song reached me and I finally stopped eating, everyone else's plate untouched. It was so beautiful. They sang in long, high notes together, "He is! He is!"

The Lord lay His head down on His clenched fist on the table. I could see His other hand on His heart because He was sitting right next to me. He was smiling and absorbing the praise with His face down.

Then, He opened up His hand and put three small stones on the table [40]. They must have been the same ones as before, smooth and beautiful. He motioned toward me and then towards Ezekiel. For a moment I looked at Him in horror because I thought He wanted me to hit Ezekiel in the head with one of them. This would have been comical if it were not so horrible.

He shook His head, trying not to laugh, as He pointed beyond Ezekiel to a tiny little hole in the wall. I saw in the spirit how some of the praise was leaking out of that hole before it had a chance to be absorbed by the Lord. He wanted me to plug it up one of the stones. I arose slowly, so as not to disturb the other two and put the stone in the hole. It fit perfectly.

Jesus stood up after several minutes. The bench we had both been sitting on skidded the floor. He peaked out the door (but none of the praise escaped out of it) and 'stage whispered', "David, come here!" Within moments, the small figure peeped around the doorway. I smiled at him.

He came in with his harp and joined the song, adding words and melody. His fingers flew over the little instrument, the song simple, the accompaniment intricate. Praise filled the room. Jesus sat back down enraptured and still. I could not do anything but sit and watch.

THE ROAD

After only a few minutes, I got up quickly, excitedly announcing, "I have to go find other people who are hungry to taste this wonderful food! Please excuse me." I did not know if there were any that were hungry in the City of God. I didn't know if there would even be enough food or if others were welcome, but I had to find out. Upon exiting the tiny house, I finally noticed a little road directly in front of it. It was thick with mud. I squatted down to it, seeing a sort of ripple in it. I dug through it like a little girl digging for periwinkles at the beach.

To my astonishment, a hand grabbed me. It was terrifying! I knew where I was, however, and gathered to myself that it must be something I was suppose to do. I pulled and pulled. It was a man's hand! I finally pulled the man out of the mud. He sat there, both of us out of breath, looking around. His eyes suddenly became wide as if fear had swept over him, "No! No! This is not where I want to be at all!" He jumped back into the mud and it swallowed him whole.

I reached down for him, grabbing his hand with all my might. I could hear him screaming as he dangled between Earth and Heaven. I held onto his slippery arm with great strength. "Let me go!" He was trying to wiggle and kick his way out of my hold!

"Let him go, Amy!" The Lord was standing sternly beside me.

"No! I can't! He has to live!" I pulled with all my might, each finger slipping from my hold.

The Lord bent down beside me, my face wet with sweat, my eyes dripping tears. He softly said to me, "He isn't a lost one." I was confused.

This was not a salvation I was pulling through?

"He's saved..." I was trying to pull him into the city!

I child of God not wanting to see this? Then what had he been crying for? Surely his hands were up here for a reason.

"He does not want to be changed." I looked at the Lord in stillness.

How could he not want this? Could the Lord be right? Yes....

I let go of the man. He fell down with a sigh back to Earth. I was sobbing.

Then, I saw more hands, straight in front of me, there must have been a dozen of them, reaching. These had already broken through the road and were reaching hard for someone to pull them up! I made my way to the closest one. I pulled with all my might. A dear friend came through the mud. The mud clung to his blonde hair. He was happy to see me and I was thrilled to see him. I couldn't wait to show him everything. But, much to my astonishment, after only ten seconds of sitting there, catching his breath, he said, "Well, I have to go back now to minister." Before I could answer, he flung himself back into the soft spot he came out of and was gone.

I looked towards the next person's hands, utterly confused. I pulled that person up as well. I didn't recognize this one. He just looked around, and disappointedly said, "Oh, I thought I was reaching for prosperity." And without another word of explanation, threw himself back into his hole.

The next one I pulled up, I was beginning to lose strength, feeling like I was going to burst into tears at any moment. I grabbed hold and out came a dear person to me I had wounded a long time ago. I had tried to make things right, but it seemed nothing I had done had been sufficient. He took one look at me and spit directly into my face. The world seemed to stop with that crushing blow. He didn't even look around. *I* was here and that was enough information for him. He jumped back in his hole and vanished as well. My heart was broken.

Then, through my agony of tears, I saw two little hands reach for me directly behind me where I was sitting. "I can't do this again." I heaved slowly. However, I girded myself up and yanked with all my might to those little arms. Out came my little five year old girl, Cora. Her little arms embraced me, as we sat there crying.

"Mommy, Mommy!" She squealed. I felt something latch onto my leg. I pulled up my leg and with it came my little three year old boy, Christian. He held onto me, too. We just sat there in the mud crying our eyes out. An angel appeared and took Cora's hand.

I stood up with Christian in my arms. The road had ended here and it led to a marble building. It had an open air walkway in the middle of it. It was a catacomb. We went through the aisle. In the middle of the building on my left, we noticed a small picture of Christian's birth mother who passed away in Russia. I small red flower was there as well. I kissed her picture and so did Christian. A healing moment for both of us.

Then, an angel came to take care of Christian. She was specially designed and chosen for him. I realized that angels were *assigned* to the children on Earth as well. They were waiting in Heaven until they were each born.

The other angel appeared again with Cora in her arms. Cora touched her lips as she talked. The angel handed her over to me and we jumped up and down together, all of the mud disappearing off of us. We were wiped clean with joy. Cora willingly went back to the angel again as I was ushered into a small shop on the other side of the narrow, mud street.

THE SIGN

The shop was filled with hats and gloves. A place to sit with a small mirror was in the middle of the shop with glass displays all around. I picked out a plain, brown cowboy hat with a tan strap. My opera gloves went all the way up to my elbows and did not seem to match the design of the hat. I looked in the mirror and noticed my hair was getting a lighter color, possibly from being outside so much.

I walked out of the store and a small boy greeted me. I knelt down to talk with him. "My name is Jacob," he chirped. He was so jovial!

"I have something for you," I heard myself say, not knowing why. I reached in my pocket and pulled out a sort of nut. It almost looked like a shark's tooth, but it curled in at the sharp point. "It's a seed." *It is?* I thought after I said it.

Jacob took the seed from my hand and started digging. Beside the place where I had pulled my children from the mud, he planted the odd seed. Then, he covered it back up with the rich dirt. "Sing to me!" He demanded as a little child would at bedtime. I sang the song imbedded deep within me:

"Fairest, Lord Jesus
Ruler of all nature.
Oh Thou of God and man the Son,
Thee will I cherish,
Thee will I honor
Thou my soul's glory, joy and crown. [36]"

I sang verse after verse, my voice becoming stronger with each word. Then, on the verse I had saved until last, I heard Jacob's voice join in with me, "Beautiful Savior..." My voice became like his little voice as we sang as one.

The song filled the air like smoke and then liquidized. It poured onto the little seed's nest with great care. When the song was over, Jacob said, "That is the song I needed. I will sing it here and water your tree. When you come back here, when your life on Earth is through, you will see a beautiful red tree. Then you will know that your faith is real and what happened to you here is real." My praise will water my faith.

THE FIRE

I walked back to Ezekiel's house, the Lord very near me as I walked. Inside Ezekiel's house, I took off my gloves and hat and placed them in a basket the lady had in her hand.

"Did you find anyone to eat with us?" She asked in anticipation.

"Just my little children, but they are not old enough yet to eat meat like this– spiritual meat like this." She nodded in disappointment. I was trying to shake my own as well.

The Lord brought a chair up to the red headed lady towards the door as Ezekial and I talked close to the fire. We talked quietly, me warming my still wet clothes. It felt like it was getting darker and cooler outside and cozy in. I stood up behind the sitting Ezekiel and wrapped my arms around him in an unabashed way. He felt so much like a dear grandfather I had known my whole life. We spoke intimately as if we had that relationship our whole lives.

"You look as though you have had a hard life," I said. I realized how rude I had been, and opened my mouth to change the subject when Ezekiel reached up and touched my arm.

"Yes, I have." He seemed proud like a little boy showing me his scars.

"Ezekiel, why don't people want to come here?"

"Because, my dear, this is a place where people die." I nodded in the same knowledge. I *had* died here. But now, I was alive in Christ [41]. Who wouldn't want that? But, I had to admit, the dying was not at all fun. I sat down next to him, my feet on the opposite side of the bench, so I could talk to him face to face.

"What is the wheel inside the wheel [42]?" I asked, changing the subject.

"I don't know yet." He replied to my amazement. "I believe it is the glory of God, but I can't be sure. That revelation has not been shown me yet."

"But I thought when you die, you are shown all the mysteries of the world. We shall know face to face."

"The only One who knows everything is sitting right over there... He continues to reveal Himself to us even here. Think of the seraphim around the throne crying out 'holy, holy, holy' [43]. It is because every time they say that, a new revelation of Him is shown. It is what keeps them worshiping. He is a depth we cannot reach." Then he added in hope of an answer to the mystery of the wheels, "Have *you* asked Him?"

"Yes, but He has not answered me yet." I looked at Ezekiel's face. He must have been only about forty years old, but the weight of the world seemed to have rested on his shoulders during his time. He had lost a lot of teeth and his ears bent at the tips. "How did you lay on your side like that for like– a year?" [44]

"I prayed." I thought there would be a "better" explanation than that. He stared at the fire, thinking intently.

I was remembering what God said to Ezekiel as He gave him his prophetic anointing, "Ezekiel, I do not want anyone's blood on my hands. [45]"

"Neither do I, dear one. He will keep you, though. Do not worry. You have something better than I did."

That's what David said, I thought. I do. I have the new covenant. I have the Messiah of all messiahs. We both looked at our raw hands. No blood. I glanced back at the Love of my life. He nodded at me as He continued to talk to the woman.

"Who is she?" I finally asked Ezekiel.

"She is my sister," he said to my surprise. "She is a great comfort to me. She helps me."

"Why didn't you ask for an angel to stay with you?"

"An angel is not the same as a person— especially one related to you." I honestly didn't understand. I couldn't imagine a person being more comforting than an angel. "Angels," he continued, "do not understand pain. I went through a lot of pain in my life." I put my head down on his shoulder, facing away from the fire. I watched the Lord talking. I caught His eye and He stopped for a minute, losing His chain of thought when He saw me.

"You went through a lot of pain in your young life as well," I heard Ezekiel say as I looked away dreamily.

"That doesn't matter..." I said gazing blissfully again at Jesus.

"Of course it does! It has made you who you are. Thank God for that!" I picked my head up and looked at him.

"I do, but I have to admit that I don't ever want to go through that again."

"You won't. He will keep you. You won't have to go through the same cycle again. Remember, He's a warrior. He will war for you. He fought for me many times."

"Why did your people kill you [46]?" I asked Ezekiel.

"There is something that you have to know, my dear one, they did not hate *me*. They hated the Lord."

"That makes me more upset," I said back to him.

"It gives me peace. I know I did everything I could." Ezekiel stood up and leaned near the fire. His face changed instantly to a young one, as if a wind blew all the pain away. I felt more guarded against him, as if I didn't know him anymore. His hair was full and his face happier.

"How long have you been here?" I asked.

"A day is a thousand years and a thousand years a day. [47]"

"Just a few days?"

"Yes." I knew now why he was still healing. I always thought that the healing of emotions would happen instantly after we died.

All of a sudden, a thought I could not shake came to me. It burst out of me uncontrollably, "You know, my name means 'beloved'."

"Yes, I do. You are the greatly loved one." He seemed to know the statement was coming before I did. Somehow, it flowed with the conversation, even if it seemed out of context. "It is time you *know* who you are." He touched my cheek as a father would. *Who am I?* I thought anxiously.

I turned to leave, sensing the Lord pulling me out of the house. I turned my head a little as Ezekiel called after me. "You know, 'David' means the same thing."

"I know." I said quietly.

CHAPTER 10

THE BROTHER

I sensed that the Lord stayed in the house, still chatting to Ezekiel's sister. But, I saw Him get up with me and hold the door as I walked out. We turned out of the house onto the muddy road and stopped dead in our tracks. David was sitting up against the wall of the house by the door, under the little, open window. "What are you doing?" The Lord asked him.

"I wanted to be close to you," He answered. It reminded me of something I would do.

"You know I would come to you if you called out in the field."

"I know," he paused looking up at us. "But I wanted to see you with *her*. I love watching You with her."

The comment astounded me. How was the Lord different with me? I did not understand. But then, the answer came to me and I blurted out, "I love watching the Lord with *you*." He looked over at me and smiled, each taking in the other's mystery of love for our Maker.

"I want to be near You. I want to be near *her.*" The Lord looked at him and then me. He knew I was wanting the same thing. It felt almost awkward, my great love for David. He looked down at the ground, waiting for the Lord's answer.

We did not have to wait very long. Three horses scooped us up. I do not know how to describe the sensation. It just felt like they flung us up in the air with their snouts while running and we landed perfectly on their backs. Our clothes were also changed instantly. David and I had both been wearing damp clothes. We were both changed into long, cobalt blue robes. This all happened in just a millisecond.

We ran the horses hard through the dark hills, toward the direction I had first seen the city. We turned, though, to the right where the forest was. I was in the middle of the two of their white horses. David and I raced each other giddily. As we approached the forest, we heard the Lord call out, "Go ahead, children!"

We raced through the dense wood, turning bravely and quickly through trees and underbrush with great speed and skill. It was thrilling! We came to a sudden halt at the little creek. The horses drank ravenously. David led my horse to where his was. Our breath showed in the cold. We looked at each other and laughed.

Then, panic struck me.

"Where is the Lord?" I searched wildly.

"It's okay, He said to go on."

"No! I must find Him!" I burrowed on foot through the forest until I got back out to the open hills.

David raced behind me shouting, "Wait!" But it did not matter to me.

I saw the Lord immediately ahead. He was standing by His horse who was nibbling at the fresh grass there. I ran to Him and held Him tightly. He seemed surprised by my display. "What are you doing here, My love? I told you two to go ahead." I sobbed with relief as if I was a lost child reunited with my parents.

"She's scared of losing you, my Lord," David wisely said.

"Yes, but it is something more than that," Jesus said slowly. *How could I have fear again after all I had been through here?*

David nodded at the Lord and withdrew himself, "I better go catch the horses," he said graciously as the Lord held me close.

"You will find them in exactly the same place." Jesus pulled me away a little and looked hard at my face. "Why are you so afraid?"

"I don't know."

"Come and sit down here by me and talk to me. Why are you so afraid of loving David?" The mark had been hit in my soul so hard that I felt the arrow go through with a *thud*. "Do you not have My heart beating within you?" I nodded. "Then you do not have to be afraid to love people anymore." He paused as He searched my face.

I looked directly ahead as He continued, "You are always afraid to love people because you are afraid you will love them more than Me. But you don't have to worry about getting close to people anymore, because you will love who I love, how I love them. It's my heart that beats within you."

I looked up at Him. My biggest problem. Finally brought to the light. I didn't even know it was there. That is why I held everyone at a safe distance except Him. That is why I was never my true self with anyone but Him. I took no other gods before Him seriously [48]. The fear slipped silently from my heart as remorse floated in.

"No inappropriate affection will ever exist between you and David. You just don't understand the depth of love here. My heart inside you will never let you fall." I looked at Him and He smiled. He said slowly, "You are feeling how I feel about David. And you. I hunger to be with you and spend time with you." I understood.

David emerged from the woods again, the two white horses following him at a short distance. He had a small plant in his hand. I walked over to him, the Lord disappearing behind me. On closer inspection, I noticed he had a little, white wildflower. He pealed off the leaves around it that hid it and handed it to me.

We could hear the Lord say, "Let's set up camp here." I argued back with the Lord stating the obvious— that we had nothing with us, but was immediately hushed by my companion.

REST

We walked a little forward where the Lord used to be standing, and a beautiful campfire appeared. All around our heads a white tent was hanging, secured to the ground on the sides. It appeared in an instant. It was an open air tent with a hole in the middle, like a donut, where the fire was. The tent stretched around us, easily being able to host a battalion. I could see the stars through it's translucent material. It was cool out and there were absolutely no bugs.

Two huge mattresses appeared in front of us. They were thick, red velvet with a rich, quilted top like a posh sleeping-bag. We nestled down in them. I wondered why it was dark, when I had seen the stars before and it seemed as day. I wondered if others were sleeping as well, or if *we* saw the night because we needed the rest. My mind swarmed with questions, but one was the chief of all of them.

David put his arm behind his head and looked towards me. My feet were near his head, our mattresses a few feet away from each other. His head was close to the fire, and my head close to his feet. My faith in that moment was hanging on by a small thread. It seemed like the longer I was in the City of God, the less faith I possessed, as if it was draining me of it like a car running on gas.

"Is this real?" I asked, knowing in my spirit it was, yet, having a hard time grasping it in my mind that night.

"Could you have come up with these revelations on your own? This is realer than what you do in the flesh," he said, understanding my weaknesses. I looked up at the stars and started feeling sleepy.

"Amy, Ezekiel and I were listening to what you said on Earth about not wanting God to have to pull out his plan B for your life. You wanted plan A. The thing is... there *is* no plan B. He never *has* a plan B. There was no plan B in the garden [of Eden]. Jesus was always *the* plan. You either choose to follow Him or you do not. Those who are saved and choose not to follow him, do not follow His plan. You either are in His plan, or you're not. I think Ezekiel shared that with you, too, and you forgot."

He was right, I had forgotten that he said that, but I remembered it now. I looked back up at the stars. David was closing out this very long day. I realized that I hadn't really slept since the bath house. I had learned a lot since then. It did feel like a thousand years... We reached for each other's hands at the same time, meeting barely in the middle. I looked at his smiling face. "I waited a long time for you, Amy."

"*You* waited a long time for *me*? Why would you wait on me?"

"I was waiting for you to be born and to come here. You are my sister."

"David?" I asked after a while, still holding his hand, "Did you ever ask God 'why me'? I mean, not to be rude, but why would He choose you?"

"Every day of my life. I still ask that question. Even after Samuel anointed me and prophesied that I would be king, it was difficult to believe. Right after that happened, I went right back out into the fields to shepherd some more. I didn't feel like a king there, nor was there seemingly any hope that I would be one from that view point. I thought maybe Samuel was just a crazy old man." I laughed a little. I wanted to tell him that I saw Samuel, but thought not to interrupt.

He continued, "Then, when I was in the caves, it was a very difficult time for me. It was hard for me to take the crown from my best friend (Jonathan)."

"You weren't in a hurry to be king."

"Not at all. God gave me supernatural love for King Saul, you remember. I just kept hoping that he would turn." I knew the feeling. God had asked me if I wanted someone's mantel once who didn't want it and I begged and pleaded with God for it not to be taken from that person [49].

He moved onto his side, thinking of what else to say. He continued, "Yea, I remember every day thinking 'who do I think I am', you know. I'm the youngest of my family, like you, right? Don't ever discount yourself because of that, though. Joseph's life gave me a lot of hope with that, even though he wasn't the absolute youngest. All God needed was a shepherd. So here I am."

I looked at him. He didn't seem the prima donna I pictured. He was so much humbler than any king I'd ever read about. I sighed. We fell asleep then, our hands latched together tightly.

As morning approached, I stretched and started waking up. An angel appeared at my side and helped me up. She unlatched an invisible door that I imagine had been right beside me the whole time. I stepped into the door. It was in a dressing room. The angel quickly bathed and dressed me. She put me in a light-pink gown with silver threads throughout. It was a heavy tapestry material. Then, in quick skill I had never seen on Earth, she fashioned my hair back in an elaborate way. She ushered me quickly out the invisible door and shut it behind me.

I stood there, completely dressed and ready within just a few minutes. David looked up at me, just waking up himself and smiled. "I see you brought your entourage with you," he teased me. I shook my head, my eyes wide in unbelief. "We better get going," he said, uncovering himself and jumping out of bed hurriedly.

He whistled lightly for our horses who came galloping up immediately. "Shouldn't we take this down?" I asked about the tent.

"Oh, we have 'people' for that," he said, swinging up on his horse next to me. It was funny.

We galloped back to town and got off our horses just at the entrance of the city where Ezekiel's house was. Jesus was waiting there. "Did you two have a good time?" He asked.

"Oh, yes!" It had felt so good to talk to another human being so very plainly. But it felt even better to be back in the arms of the Lord.

"I have to go." David said, looking at me with tears in his eyes. I swung myself to him, embracing him as he kissed my head. I let go of him, then changed my mind and hugged him tightly again. He kissed the back of my head again.

"Oh, stop it you, two!" Jesus insisted smiling. "You *will* see each other again." Ahh, but it was difficult to leave him.

BACK IN THE CITY

"We need to stop by Ezekiel's house and get your gloves and hat." I started to knock on the door. "Go ahead in, they're expecting you." I pushed the door open slowly. They were both milling around, getting ready for the day. Ezekiel looked up at me with even more youthfulness than he had the night before standing near the fire.

"Well, I see a good night sleep did you a world of good!"
I said, giving him a hug.

"Didn't it though?" his sister said agreeably, she looking
better as well. "Here are your gloves and your hat." She
held out the basket for me. I slipped on the long, white opera
gloves and wiggled my fingers in their place.

"I can't imagine what these are for," I said.

We walked out of the house and down the street. The
mud road was being paved over with some kind of concrete.
I looked concerned to the Lord. "Don't worry," He said,
"I will make another way for people to get here. *Through
you.*" I could still see the scene from the day before with all
those hands lifted through, even though they were all gone
at that moment.

THE BALL

We made our way passed the little hat shop to a larger
building. Jesus opened the door for me. A gorgeous entranceway
greeted us. It looked like something from out of an English
novel. It was the entrance to a beautiful ballroom. I could hear
an orchestra playing "So this is Love [50]". It was a song I knew
well. It is from the movie Cinderella [50] that Cora watched all
the time.

"So this is Love,
So this is Love.
So this is what makes Life mine
My hearts aglow,And now I know,
The keys to our Heaven are mine..." [50]

We each picked out a small flower from a table to either
hold or place on our lapels. We entered the room. It was
alive with beautiful dresses and waltzing. Jesus danced with

me. The other men wore black tuxedos, but the Lord wore His beautiful white robes still. The ladies swept gracefully around us. I felt like I was floating. At the end of the song, we went over to a high counter. The Lord ordered a sweet drink for me that I sipped.

We went back out to the dance floor, but was immediately interrupted by a well-mannered gentleman. He had black, slicked-back hair and a protruding nose. He was about the same size as I. I was not use to all these shorter men, I was a small thing, myself. He acted like a very rich, well-educated debutante without a hint of snobbery. He asked to dance with me, His eyes twinkling as He spoke with the Lord. They definitely knew each other very well. They seemed to have a secret plan between them.

He danced with me as he talked, "I am Paul." I was speechless! *Could it be the same one?* That is all he said to me. As we danced, a surge of joy flooded my entire being. I could hear the verse being spoke over me in the spirit by someone who had been in prison as he wrote it, "Rejoice in the Lord always. Again I say it, Rejoice! [51]" I bent over with the weight of joy encompassing me.

He let go of me and I stood in the middle of the dance floor, hunched over, weeping in joy. A spotlight shown over me, the rest of the ballroom silent and dark. All eyes were on me. They all wanted to see this! I couldn't stop. The Lord finally came over and rescued me as the lights went to normal and the orchestra began to play.

As we walked away, we talked. He knew my thoughts before I felt like I actually thought it, "Why are you in such a hurry to leave Me?" He asked candidly.

"I'm not, Lord, I am just anxious to write all that is happening to me so that I do not lose any of it."

"I will keep you."

THE LION AND THE LAMB

He led me outside where there was a long porch upstairs and downstairs. We walked up a flight of stairs to the second story porch where we could view more of the city. But, my mind and heart were only fixed on one place– the hillside. I stared off into the distance, searching the area for David. I saw him as a small speck quite far away. I stared out towards him as the Lord talked. I wasn't listening. He stopped in mid-sentence and said, "You miss him already, don't you."

"I have to apologize to you, Lord, but I do."

"Let's go see him," He said. I jumped a little in excitement. We left the beautiful ball and all its companions for the trek out to the field. I put my hat on for the walk. After a long walk, David saw us coming and walked up happily to embrace me.

He's as glad as I am, except I would have been running towards him, I thought in blissful amusement. My clothes changed to the dark blue robes again when I touched David. The Lord lingered nearby as we talked. I sat facing him, away from the sheep, chewing on a long piece of grass. It was sweet and calming.

Suddenly, David looked passed me in excitement. "Do you have those three small stones still?" I took them out of my pocket. There were still three. God must have replaced the one I used already in Ezekiel's house. I looked at them and then looked behind me to where David was staring. A lion! A male lion with a mane! The lion was walking amongst the sheep and lambs. I grasped onto the stones and looked back at David.

"I-I-I don't have a sling shot..." He nodded *no*. I looked closer at the behavior of the lion. "I thought that the female was the hunter. This one doesn't look like he's hunting... David, this is not a bad thing, this is a good thing! The lion lays down with the lamb up here!" I looked back over at him with this new revelation.

He looked at me dumbfounded and said, "Yes, Amy, I know..."

I got it! "It's the Lord!" I didn't see Jesus anywhere. The lion was the Lord. He came closer and leaped over the little stream in front of us. He nudged a little lamb along as He came closer to us. I opened my hand with the stones. Why had David asked if I had these if he knew this was the Lord all along?

I didn't realize how close the great Lion had gotten and suddenly I felt Him take one great *lick* at the palm of my hand with the stones in it. Then, He silently crept away the same way He had come. We both held our muscles tightly as we watched Him go.

"He was anointing the stones," David said to me. He was anointing my stones for battle.

At a distance, I watched in awe as the Lion started turning into a man. The left side of the Lion was the last to evolve into the Man Jesus. He walked back over to us, David and I both amazed. He casually came back the same way as He did as the Lion, and lay down on the grass next to me. David and I lay there as well, looking up in silence.

Then, like a lightning bolt it hit me. I sat up and looked at both of them, "The Lion lays down with the lamb! I'm a lamb!" David and Jesus both burst out laughing. "What?" I said blankly to the two warriors. "And the little child will play near the viper's nest....that means that children will not be hurt by Satan anymore!" They both laughed a little more. I felt dumb not to have realized this before. "Wow!" I whispered next to the two laughing men. [52]

They were both laughing there, mirrored images of each other. Jesus with His left arm under His head and David with his right arm under his head. It was really amazing. Even their little mannerisms were the same. I touched both of their ankles. They chuckled to a stop and looked at me. "I'm so honored..." I whispered, understanding finally the gravity of the event I was witness to. I was sitting between King David and King Jesus. It was phenomenal.

But there was something, maybe it was the twinkle in His eyes, that drew me to lean towards the right where Jesus was. I reached up and held both of their hands. I leaned my elbow on the Lord's chest and put my ear to Him. I couldn't hear a heartbeat. *How strange*, I thought.

"Remember, you have My heart," He said, even though I hadn't vocalize my thoughts. It started sinking deep in me at that point. I looked at His face. There was something about it that was so beautiful... I felt my left hand being slightly rubbed by a thumb. It was David's thumb and he was watching us. I smiled back. It felt like our time was at an end together.

I looked back at the Lord, who I felt even more drawn to at this point. I stood up with Him, just staring at His face. What was it about Him? I think it was His expressions. He sometimes looks almost bashful, sometimes determined, sometimes happy, sometimes even angry. But there's something about His face that always looks shamelessly in love.

I remembered David, who's hand I had let go of inadvertently. I turned back around quickly and looked at him, standing close behind, smiling a knowing smile. He knew this was "it" as well. He acted like he wasn't sure what to do. I threw myself on him and hugged him and dared to kiss his rosy cheek. "My sister..." he whispered and then gulped. I didn't look at him while I pulled away. I focused on the face of Jesus when I turned and walked towards Him as He walked slowly backward.

The Lord asked me a question, "Why haven't you told anyone of the crown you have been wearing on your head? I gave it to you right before we rode the horses."

"I didn't want anyone to think of me as..." I didn't have to finish. He nodded, knowing my thoughts.

"I gave it to you." I nodded in understanding.

CHAPTER 11

ANOTHER CAVE

He held my hand as we walked down and up the many green hills together. On the back of one of the hills was a small entrance way. A cave. We slipped into it and stood in a large, round, natural room in the cave. Crystals were dripping and forming on the ceiling. The little stream ran into the little cave. There, in the middle of the room, I saw another one of it's sources. It was a small hole in the ground about one or two feet in diameter. The Lord told me to spiritually put my cup in that hole of water. He told me there was no end to it. It kept reaching farther and farther in depths. I pondered this for a little while.

Then, He took me to the side of the cave where there was an old wooden door. It looked like the Lord would have to crouch a little to get in, but it was just my size. He put His hand on the latch to open it and I stopped Him. Fear surged through me. "What is behind the door, Amy?" He asked. I shook my head, I did not want to know. It would be something very frightening, I told myself, like the other cave in the City of God. I couldn't trust Him. Although good came from it, I knew *He* put me through all of that, and I didn't trust Him that He wouldn't do it again.

THE CHILDHOOD

He creaked open the door. I shut my eyes. Would I be falling in a massive abyss? What was going to happen? My eyes finally grew tired of being shut and I squinted in the light of what I was looking into. It was my old room! I sighed and almost danced with relief. The room I grew up in! It radiated pink from the walls, the furnishings, even the carpet. It was glowing softly from the little carousel lamp that hung over my little window seat. I squealed with delight as I had the first time I saw it over twenty years ago.

The Lord sat on the window seat as He watched me survey the stuffed animals still crouching around, waiting to be held. "This is where you met Me...." He said, pondering the thought tenderly. "Late at night, when everyone else was asleep, you would sing and dance in here– just for Me. I would hold your hand and walk around and around in circles in here every night with you." I blushed at the thought again. I had since grown into inhibitions of what a respectable lady should do.

I remembered almost every night, after hours and hours of prayer and especially praise, ministering to my Savior, I would collapse and sleep until the next day. Sometimes I would only get a few hours of sleep before school the next day because I could not leave His presence.

"I remember you coming home from college every weekend and putting on your wedding gown every night. You would twirl around in it like a little girl. And you would talk to Me, Amy." Those were moments that only He would know about. Those precious times of innocently worshiping

Him and loving Him. "I want those times back, Amy," He said quietly as I sat down next to Him.

"Lord, this is too personal," I said after moments of gazing at Him. "I can't write this down..."

"I will give you courage to write what I need you to write." He touched my cheek.

THE WINDOW

I felt the strange sensation of being lifted up and up and up, as if the roof above us did not exist. Even though I felt like we were moving upward, we were actually moving miles eastward toward the ocean. We landed on a dune where my Grandmother's house was when I was small. The ocean looked so wonderful and not another person could be seen. We looked at each other and tore off our outer robes so that just our inside garments (which were a lot like thick slips) were on us. We raced towards the water in such joy that I almost fell down. Waist deep, we jumped through the breaking waves that were almost overtaking us.

Jesus then blessed me. "I have commanded an open Heaven to be above you at all times. No matter where your feet may step, the open Heaven will be above your head. There, angels will be able to descend and ascend." I looked up, and not ten feet from my head, the sky opened up and a large hole the size of about twenty feet showed me Heaven itself. It was a glassless window to Heaven! [53]

I took a few steps away from Jesus to test it. The hole moved with me. It was like a moving window in the floor of Heaven that showed me exactly what was above my head at that given time. I saw the streets of gold. I ran a little ways and it moved over to the steps of the throne room. I ran some more until the hole was directly below the very steps to the throne of the Father. I looked up, joy flooding my every cell. Jesus was laughing behind me.

There He was! The Father looked down and peered over the window to look at me! I wanted to scream with glee, but I could do nothing. I finally forced my hand to jut out towards Him to pick me up, so great was the pull to be even nearer to Him. I thought He would pull me by the arm, but instead, He scooped me up like a baby and lay me flat on my face in front of the very stairs that lead to Him!

I could hear people all around me, their murmurings loud and sometimes bothersome. Some were pacing, some were shouting, all were pleading. I peaked and saw a middle age woman walking back and forth, her hands clasped under her chin. Her eyes were closed and on her head was a crown.

I didn't feel to do anything but just lay there, face down. I smiled from ear to ear in His presence. After a while, He scooped me up again and set me on His lap. "Few just want to be near me without wanting anything from me," He said in pleasure. I felt like a little girl again, and I probably was. I felt small, but important there with Him, sitting on the lap of my dear Father.

A thick cloud was around His head and I began to feel an unbelievable amount of curiosity. I could feel Him smiling. I reached out and touched the cloud. It felt like a soft blanket. I pulled it up from His face a little so that I could see His mouth.

He was smiling, His beautiful teeth showing. Something spark inside of me. A little more to reveal a nose. I knew Him! It was Jesus! He was a white haired, white bearded *Jesus*! I was breathless. He roared with delight. I dropped the veil and sat with my mouth wide open. Then I cried out with all of my power, "You *are* the same Person!" The revelation hit me square in the face. The theology, yes, I had gotten that, but this was *He* and the face was the same! [54]

I sat back against His arm, in awe. Why had I been so afraid of the Father all this time? He was One and the Same!

I slid down off His lap and started down a glass-like staircase that was not very high from the ocean I had come from. I walked down to the ocean where Jesus still was standing.

MY GRANDMOTHER'S HOUSE

We ran up to the dune, soaked and exhilarated. There was new clothes lay out for me. A gorgeous white gown that was made of a type of cotton that felt like silk. The Lord fashioned a wide, wrinkly, silk ribbon around my waist. It was a beautiful deep orange color. The Lord motioned for me to look up. The window of Heaven had traveled with me and I could see a small portion of the cloud of witnesses. There faces reminded me of the excitement I saw on my family's face when I thought I saw Santa Claus one Christmas. That had happened here, at my Grandmother's house.

Looking at their faces caused a longing in my heart. I ran back to the specific spot in the ocean, gathering up my beautiful dress so that it wouldn't touch the water. I stood waist deep in the waves. I looked up at the face of my Father. He smiled down at me. I stood there for a minute, just looking at Him. I eventually left, my legs itching with the feel of the salt water.

We walked down the little drive that lead from the beach to my Grandmother's house. We stopped in front of her grassy yard, looking at the house I had spent so many happy days of my childhood. There was a palm tree my Grandfather had planted before I was born in the front yard. The Lord and I played around it, still giddy from the experience on the beach.

As I was gazing breathlessly again at the front of her house, I remembered something deep in my psyche. When I was a very small child, there was a concrete wall that went around my Grandmother's backyard. Although this wall was only five feet high, I could never see over it. I would try to climb it, but would always come scurrying down, skinning my knees on the concrete ground. There were pretty little stones of pink and green that were all over the ground as well, which added to the discomfort of the fall. But I never gave up, bleeding or not.

One day, right before she passed away, I had stretched my neck and pulled myself far enough up it to see what lay beyond it. I saw the cactus, the dunes, and the beautiful waves. Although I had been to the beach every day, I had always had to walk to it some distance. This was the first time that I could squarely look from my Grandmother's yard to the ocean. I realized how very close I was to the waves. The walk to the beach, around the curvy street, had seemed endless as a toddler. But there it was, just beyond the wall! Could this be the way many people feel about closeness with God? They try to take so many long avenues to Him, when He is right there in their backyard the whole time. They have simply built a wall around themselves.

I turned around and talked to the surfer I knew behind me. The Lord commented that I, too would take up this sport soon to him. We just stood out in the street very casually talking to the neighbor. As I did, I could feel the very top layer of my garment start to lift off. (There must have been six or so layers of skirt underneath the top layer.) It finally detached itself from me and hovered like a sheet around the house and land that was my Grandmother's at one time. I had always wanted to own that house again. Then, I realized that it was making a tent and spread out all over the city that I grew up in.

Then, it spread further north along the east coast. "Your tents are expanding, [55]" the Lord said, His hair still wet with salt water. It continued up towards Washington D.C. and then started going westward.

This is where I stopped the Lord, "I have never even been to these places. How will I handle this?" I asked. I knew He was giving me some kind of ministry and I honestly didn't think I wanted.

"Wherever you walk, anointing drips off you to the land you walk on. So it will be where your tent is pitched."

HOW MUCH DO YOU LOVE ME?

God Jesus' emotions changed in front of me like a changing of the wind blowing another direction. I glanced His way. He looked serious. The air was getting cooler and it was starting to become evening around us. "I am going to make good on My promise now," He said, looking intently. "Go with Me now to the mouth of Hell." I felt as if I had been stung by a bee. Months ago He had told me that one day I was going to stand at the mouth of Hell, but I refused to believe Him. I was His flesh and blood! I was not going to such a place!

"No," I said matter-of-factly, staring off in the distance.

"Come with Me."

"No."

"Come with Me," He was looking hard at me, trying to get eye contact from me. He knew just as well as I that all I had to do was look at Him in the eye and my will would be totally void. I just couldn't say "no" to Him when I looked at His face. I didn't answer this time. I just stared off in the distance.

He changed the subject, "Let's take a little walk." I walked down the road slowly with Him as He discussed the people who had resided in each house during my child-hood. "This one, too, came to know Me because of your Grandmother. This one, too. And this one, right before this person died, she accepted Me because of your Grandma." The last one I had known well. She had been a heavy lady, beaten daily by her drunk husband. My Grandmother was always helping her.

"I never seem to know how to evangelize to someone, Lord. It always seems so awkward. Teach me how to do it."

"I will anoint you when the time is right so that it feels natural. All you have to do is love Me. I'll take care of the rest." As we were talking, we walked further on the circular road until we were right in front of my Grandma's house again. I looked up at His wonderful face. He did not forget, "Go with Me to Hell, Amy." He got me.

A startling thing came from my lips, "I am the Lord's handmaiden. Be it done unto me according to Thy Word." And with that statement came a deep sense of foreboding. But I added in faith, "No matter where You go, I will go. As long as I may be with You."

"No matter the pain?"

"No matter. I am already dead." I honestly could not believe that just came out of me. Who was this person talking? My flesh could not fight her any longer. I remember thinking, *the anointing does crazy things to a person.*

He looked upward in the distance, seemingly pleased with me. "Not yet, though, you're not ready. In two days I will take you. Be sensitive and vigilant as to when I call you quietly."

CHAPTER 12

INTERMISSION

I went back instantly to Earth. I opened my blurry eyes and just sat for a while. I tried to eat, not because I was hungry, but just to feel like I had skin on again. I needed to feel human. It was a strange sensation.

For two days, I was a beast. "Maybe God will change His mind," I reasoned. "What purpose could this possibly serve?" I complained. "My journal is so beautiful, this is going to mar it greatly! Why can't I just focus on His beautiful face?" I sinned.

I ignored the Lord for two full days.

Finally, at the end of the second day, no one could stand living with me any longer. I sat down in a humph in the big armchair. The voice of God, "If you do not stop ignoring Me, you are going to die. I am Your Healer and Deliverer." Within seconds I was in the spirit.

THE GATES OF HELL CANNOT PREVAIL

I repented and fell back into His arms. In the embrace, we fell fast into a blazing furnace. My hair stuck straight up, so quick was our descent. "Why are we not burning up?" I yelled to the Lord over the roar of the fire.

"Fire cannot quench or burn up love. It is the only thing that does not burn up." He yelled back.

We fell onto a type of floor, our feet landing perfectly, keeping our balance. I realized later that this "floor" was the gate, or mouth of Hell. It was enormous- it went farther than I could see. It was made of hairless human heads, decapitated and "planted" by their necks in a human excrement-type of glue that made up the entire gate. There were millions and millions. I took a few steps, sloshing in the mud-like substance. I tried not to step on any heads and I found a small area to just stand for a minute in the dung. As I did, both the Lord and I fell through the disgusting substance like it swallowed us up.

We were suddenly in a glass-like tube. It seemed more like the substance they put on aquariums for whales– it was so thick. I clung to the Lord as we descended again very quickly. I hated the feeling, but we were protected. The tube stopped and these beings, who I think were women, ran towards us and threw themselves almost through the glass. They kept throwing themselves again and again onto it. I could hear their screams. They sounded exactly like my little daughter, crying out in agony for me. "What are they doing?" I wept in terror.

"They are trying to get a drop of water. I am the River they thirst for. [56]"

"Oh, God!" I buried my face in His chest.

We landed on something soft. The glass protecting us vanished and I looked up with eyes wide and terrorized. A being was towering over us. He was lobster-like in color.

He had two large claws for arms. The rest of him was hard to explain. He seemed to have an exoskeleton like an ant. His mouth was like an ant's as well. I could not look farther than his mouth in fear. He was inches from me, leaning over me as I clung to Jesus.

Satan. "I will rip your children to shreds!" he was yelling. "What you saw was nothing! The deepest part of Hell is the part that I, myself, enjoy the most. It is the place where I will one day put you! It is the place I put all Christians who fall away. I torture them there myself, day and night. It brings me great pleasure."

He's lying. God will not let me go. He will not let us go. [57] *No place like that exists,* I told myself. But I didn't speak.

"Why are you here, Nazarene?" But the Lord didn't answer him. Realizing the dreadful mistake Satan had made in his lunatic anger, he quickly changed himself into a being easier to trust. He became in, an instant, a small, white haired monk. He put his hands together as if in prayer and bowed to me and said, "Please, follow me."

The Lord put His arm around me and firmly turned us and lead me in the opposite direction. Satan slithered back into his original form, his sense dulled by rage once again, and came directly in front of us. He was panting in fury. I looked at the Lord. The Master had a small smirk on His face. What was He doing? Why was He picking a fight like this?

Satan started on his blasphemous tyrant: "Why do you come down here? Because you like it just as much as I do!"

I looked deep into the Master's face and asked, "Why can't you just kill him now and be done with all this?" I asked in a meek voice.

Satan looked at me and back at the Lord. There was a look of shear terror on his face that I cannot even begin to try to describe. The Bride just asked the Bridegroom, who adores her, to do away with her enemy once and for all. And in that moment, because he cannot understand prophecy, Satan believed He would do it.

The Lord's reply was steady. "I cannot destroy spirit. Satan is a spirit just like you have a spirit. Besides, I enjoy the competition." He was making fun of Satan.

Satan's ant-like mouth grew wide and smiled almost larger than his entire body's length. His teeth seemed to be ten feet across. "You like it down here, don't you?" Satan continued. "You would have destroyed this place a long time ago if you didn't love evil and rebellion as much as I do! In fact, you and I are a lot alike...Hey, what makes you think you can even come into my domain in the first place! I own you here! I can do whatever I want with her here because I own this place!"

The Lord smiled slyly. He reached in His pocked and pulled out old fashioned keys on a large hoop. Satan saw them and fell back in terror. He had forgotten that the Lord had the keys for Hell as well.

I got the revelation and immediately found myself on my Grandmother's front lawn again. I caught my breath. I lay down on the St. Augustine grass, coughing and trying to get a hold of myself. "I spared you from much," He said, sitting next to me.

"I know," I said. "I thought it would be much worse."

"It is. I am only going to show you what I need to show you."

"I am thankful for that."

CHAPTER 13

The next day, I opened my eyes on the beach where I had grown up. I saw the Lord pacing beside me. He had somehow moved me many yards down to the shore line where I was lying. "What's the matter?" I asked, not use to seeing the Lord with concern on His face.

"I dread taking you today..."

"I know, but I must know what you need to tell me." The fear was gone.

(I remembered not long ago when the Lord had taken me in the spirit to a beautiful hill. There He had angrily wept at me. I did not believe in Hell at the time. I remembered His words, "When you deny that Hell exists, you deny that this pain that I have exists. You say to me, 'You're not suffering, because this place does not exist.' But I tell you that when one of my little ones is thrown in there, do I not weep and weep?" He had trailed off in tears so bitterly He couldn't breathe. It was for my own comfort that I had not believed. I had never taken in consideration the suffering He was going through.)

He looked at me and told me to be strong. I nodded and we returned. It was literally more than I could bare. The Lord knew it and dropped us down to another level, getting us through the experience as quickly as possible. We were plunged into a murky water. Bodies were floating around in it. The Lord gave me ability to breath, but these people were drowing for all eternity. A wrecked ship lay just behind them with open treasure chests full of gold and jewels. In fact, most of them still had necklaces around their necks that looked like they were easily worth millions each. "Greed," the Lord told me.

We moved quickly on into another dimension, above water. There was eery music and clowns and other faces were popping up all around me. Different works of art were coming up from all sides, the tile floor seemed to be moving. It was just chaos. I prayed, "Lord, please protect my mind." I thought I was going insane. All around, the images were coming up too quick to even understand what I was seeing.

The music was thrown together as if a great orchestra was all playing different music. It sounded horrible. The colors, the light! It was too much. I was literally losing my mind. "Creative expression without divine impression." The Lord spoke and it stopped. I was starting to understand. Faint remembrances of Dante's Inferno crashed through me. *He had a vision of this!* I gasped. There are different parts of Hell for the different sins.

Just as quickly as that revelation came, we were dropped into another dimension. Less than a foot in front of us was a huge castle. It was horrid looking, like it was made of dung that had dried into this monstrosity. It looked a lot like the dribble castles we made at the beach, but black and foul. We started to climb it. I could hear the flap of a gigantic bat's wings close behind us. The wind picked up my hair a little as I climbed higher, never losing my footing. He could not intimidate me.

He finally appeared directly above us, pulling himself up backwards towards the opening we were aiming for. He was scared to death and tried in vain to convince us that we had no power here. We pulled ourselves up through the open balcony where Satan had already gotten to steps before us. He was cowering in a corner. He looked like an ordinary, naked demon, shivering there, trying not to look at us. I stood there feeling like a well-trained General on the winning side.

"GET BACK!" The Lord roared as our feet touched the floor. Satan was thrown by His power to the opposite side of the room and slammed against the wall. He was knocked out. "I did this to show you that we can go to the enemy's *house* and tell *him* what to do. " I smiled. "I have one more thing to show you before we leave this place."

We quickly started ascending. On our way back out, we stopped. There was a huge cage with an enormous bear in it. His teeth were huge and very sharp, grotesquely deforming his face. He looked at me and leaped towards me. I backed away a little. He was in what looked like an old circus cage. He was torturing himself. With his massive claws, He was scratching and scratching his back until part of his coat would come up.

As he tugged at his fur, it started coming up like a costume would. But this bear was real! I could see a human's back underneath the coat on his back. I asked the Lord what I was seeing. "This is the demon you have been coming up against. I had you bind him and here he is." The bear screamed wildly. That thing had been loose! I'm glad I had not seen it until now. No wonder that thing was so hard to get rid of.

"This was the stronghold you were under," the Lord said without emotion. I gulped. When had I fought this thing?

The bear began to talk. He tried to manipulate me by changing his voice. He sounded sweet, like someone dear to me, "Open my cage," he began. "Why are you keeping me in here? I want to get out of here. Please..." How did he think he could seduce me now? I saw him so clearly.

"He controlled you for quite some time," the Lord said emphatically. "But now he's caged. This is the spirit of Control."

POST TRAUMA

I blinked and I was back on the beach. I opened my eyes as the little waves washed over my legs. I thought for a moment that the waves were black and I was back in Hell again. I panicked and started scrambling away from the lava water. The Lord touched my left arm lightly. I saw clearly for a moment or two and then flashed back again. This went on and on for a while. It slowed down finally as I focused on the Lord.

My ear was full of wet sand as I lay there with my head turned towards Him. I was lying on my stomach and gasping for air. He just kept touching me to bring me back to Him. Too much. Too much to ever write was seen. And I just lay there, counting every pore on His face. I blinked slowly and started returning to normal.

He finally helped me up and I wobbled on my weak legs. I started feeling strengthened. The entrance to the cave appeared. He led me back through it. I looked around. David's things were scattered around as if he had been in there while we were gone.

"David," I whispered longingly. The well was still there, I had forgotten about it, in the middle of the room. I drank from a small bucket that had dove deep into it to get me water. I felt more like myself and the Lord brought me back into the beautiful sunshine of the shepherd's field outside the city.

CHAPTER 14

BACK IN THE CITY

My eyes hurt in the light, coming out of the cave. I squinted to look around at the quaint little stream going into the hidden cave. I searched for David. No sign of him. I clung to the Lord. He had trouble walking with me clinging to Him. We entered the city limits and stepped unto the beautiful, gold-bricked road on a street

We turned left at the first building we saw. It was a small building like the ones we had been in where the Tabernacle was. It was another jewelry store- this one filled with diamond jewelry. I looked at the Lord quizzically as to say, "Why are we in another jewelry store? I don't even like jewelry."

I scanned the store quickly, not really caring what I was seeing, ready to move on already. The unbelievably expensive jewelry was just laying out everywhere. It wasn't organized under the glass like the silver store was. There was shelves all the way around the little store where these million dollar pieces were just thrown all over.

I caught a small movement on a bottom shelf in front of me. My eyes seemed to open again to reveal another layer of what I was seeing. A huge, brown snake was slithering there. It was printed like a rattle snake, but bigger, with no rattle. He was pushing around the jewelry. His head was moving a small, diamond tiara.

I ran behind the Lord, who was also standing in the store. Upon doing that, I felt a nudge on my back. I swooped around to see another snake doing the same thing. The shelves were covered with them, slowly pushing around the jewelry! I screamed shortly. I looked down in horror. Under my feat were snakes slithering as if the floor was alive!

The Lord stood almost motionless, unmoved by the horrific display. He handed me a small orb. It was heavy like solid glass in my hand. I started speaking, *"You may have bruised His heal, but He has crushed your head!* [58]*"* Light flew out of the orb and disintegrated all the snakes instantly!

As we walked out of the store I asked the Lord what the snakes meant. How could they have infiltrated into the City of God? "You brought them here, Amy. They are the judgements you have put on people. I have tried to give my people their special gifts, but you have held Me up in intercession because you judged them." I asked for forgiveness immediately and walked to the next building.

THE CIRCUS

We entered a huge building across the street. It was as big as a conference center. I could hear the yells of the crowd. I looked up and there was a trapeze artist doing stunts way up high on a swing. A circus. "Why are we here, Lord?" I moaned. "I *hate* circuses!" I sat down with Him in a huff on the front row. Someone was giving out popcorn and I motioned for one. I snacked away, humped over and pouting.

"Let's go in there," The Lord told me. I put my popcorn down and got up with Him. I hadn't been in a horrible mood in the city until that day. Something was really bothering me, but I hadn't uncovered it yet. For the moment, my main concern was getting out of this ridiculous circus as quickly as possible. But, there was something I had to see apparently. We walked right into the little gate between the audience and the main dirt pit.

"I don't want to go in there," I said like a teenager grumbling.

"Too bad," He said quietly as the circus announcer met us with a top hat on. He greeted us happily as if we owned the place (or at least the Lord owned it). A man with a chair was "taming" a male lion in the middle of the arena. The Lord and I walked up to the lion. The Lord started petting him casually like he was His dog. I reached out and did the same while the Lord talked gently to the lion tamer. I really got into it and scratched the lion under his chin. The animal was really enjoying it.

I heard the lion tamer remark to the Lord, "Well I guess You really ruined that stunt. You can't tame a very tame lion."

I looked up at the acrobats. They let go of the handles of the swing when they saw the Lord and flew down to Him. They commented to the Lord, "Well I guess you really ruined that stunt. There's no intrigue now that the audience knows You've already given us the ability to fly."

I looked ahead of me just in time to see a huge elephant running towards me, his great tusks looking like they were going to "get" me at any moment. The Lord pushed me towards the elephant. The sweet elephant stopped right in front of me and started touching me gently with his trunk, like he was giving my face kisses. On that note, we left.

I sighed, "Well, Lord, at least there was no clowns..."
The Lord motioned to the audience, filled with clown faces.
I shook my head.

Could this be the universal church? Could this be the
Body of Christ doing their stunts? What could this all mean?
I pondered this for a while. Maybe a lot of what we do *is* for
show, not to display His awesome power, but *ours.* We put
on masks and fool around.

I loved the lion and the elephant, though. They represented the strength of the Lord. At least there was *something*
to get out of this "service" they were conducting.

TEN BOOM RESIDENCE

We left the circus and went down the street a few yards
and then across the street. The Lord stood by a small house
a lot like Ezekiel's and knocked. I smiled at Him. He looked
a lot like the portrait of Him I had always loved as a child,
knocking on the door of someone's heart.

"Who lives here, Lord?" I asked. Immediately, the door
opened to reveal one of the most beautiful sights I had ever
seen. An old, unattractive woman opened the door.

"Corie!" I gasped. "That's Corie Ten Boom!" I squeaked
out. I was star struck. She let me in congenially. Inside was
her sweet sister, Elizabeth, and their elderly father. I stood,
not knowing what to do.

As we made our "hello's", the Lord said, "Corie, Amy
named her daughter after you."

"Ohh..." Elizabeth chirped happily. We sat down at
the table together, their father next to me on the bench we
shared.

"I miss you," I said to Corie. "I know I never met you
before, but I feel that I know you from your books. I miss
women like you in the world."

Corie said, "Aren't you going to let Him in?" She motioned for Jesus, still standing in the open doorway.

"No," I heard myself say. I was in shock. "I am mad at Him." *I was? Where was this coming from? Some depth that God was digging into me to uncover that which I had tried to cover up? Why was this coming out now?* Corie looked at me in shock and a little angrily. I felt an attitude attach itself to me.

"Why are you mad at the Lord?" Elizabeth asked, almost in tears.

"You can't be mad at Him, Amy. He's the only One who can help you," Corie said sternly. Corie got up and lead the Lord into the room to sit at the head of her table.

"Why are you angry with Me, Amy?" The Lord asked gently.

"Because You will not answer my prayer."

"What prayer is that?"

"Please, Lord, please!" I moaned, "Do something to rescue North Korea!" I pleaded with all that was inside me. It had been my heart's cry out to Him for a while.

The Lord banged angrily on the table as He stood up. "I told you not to touch that until I told you to! [59]"

"I am the Bride and I am asking You!" I yelled back.

"You do not *get* to lead! You get to *follow*! I have not told you to pick that up yet!" He yelled forcefully at me. It was the first time I had ever heard Him angry with me. Yes, He had told me numerous times not to start praying for that country until He released me to, but it wasn't fair how long He was taking! There were concentration camps in huge numbers over there! The people were suffering so.

I finally realized where I was and how I had acted. I stood up in shame, embarrassment and angered, as I ran out of the house. I kept running down the road and went to the green hills where David watched his sheep. I kept running until I found him. I called to him, but when he turned around, my hero's face was distorted with a memory that was haunting me of him. The memory of the scriptures that told how he ruthlessly killed women and children. I backed away from him in horror.

The little stream looked more like a little ditch to me. Everything around me was changing in a terrible way. The colors all started to fade to grays. Realizing it was my only chance, I threw myself into the low little river.

"Clean me, Holy Spirit! I know I am wrong!" I soaked myself in the shallow water. Grieving unashamed, the tears dripped harder than the river flowed. It took me a couple of seconds to realize it, but a gentle hand was on my back. I whimpered up and held the Lord's hand as He lead me back into the Ten Boom house. I stood there, dripping and sniffling. "I am so ashamed!" I let out a long wail.

"There is no shame here," Corie said forcefully. I had so wanted to show Corie and her family how very spiritual I was. Now they were seeing the horrible side of me that I didn't even realize was there. I was so shocked and embarrassed with myself. I wanted God to press the rewind button, but it was too late. I wept bitterly, but the Lord would not let me leave again. I sat down in a chair.

Why wouldn't the Lord let me intercede for North Korea? I was hysterical. I could see flashes of my bedroom back home, it's light blue walls and antique mirrors. "Stay with me!" Corie had her hand on my cheek, looking almost nose to nose with me. I wanted to go home. "Stay with me!" She said again and I relaxed back into the spirit realm with her again. I started calming down, but I was exhausted.

A large cradle-like bed was in the corner of the room. I hadn't noticed it before. It looked like a tarnished, silver, pea pod, big enough for a grown person to crawl inside of. Elizabeth helped me in. I felt myself shrink down to a small infant inside of the cradle. I heard Elizabeth's sweet voice say, "God, she has the heart of a missionary," she had said it with a sigh. I wondered if she thought that was a bad thing.

"I need to speak with you outside," Corie said as she took the Lord's arm and lead Him outside to the street. (I suppose she had a little conference with Him.)

I opened my eyes and saw a rocking chair in front of me. In it, rocking and watching me was the Father. I couldn't really make out His whole face. He looked like a blurred memory. He scooped me up and held me to His chest. I was a tiny infant again, learning who He was all over again.[60] My sobs were muffled by His large chest. I said inside myself to Him, "Can't you help them, Lord?"

"You know, Amy. You are so much like Me... We both want everything to be right and good right now." He was so loving. He looked at my little face. "From the moment you were a little girl and started crying at night in guilt... you would cry because even at a very young age you realized how much you had and how little others had. I heard you then, crying out to Me. And I hear you now. But what you have to grasp is my timing. We must be patient with My timing."

I must have fallen asleep. I awoke to the same steady, warm hand touching my back in the silver pea pod. I came out of my little cocoon, an adult again. I stood up and smiled at the Lord Jesus. He smiled back.

THE TRAIN

"Amy..." I looked over to Corie's dear father standing beside me. I remembered how in the book Corie asks her father how she was going to have the strength to endure what God called her to endure. He reminded her of when she was a little girl and she was going to get on a train. He would wait until the last second to give her the ticket so that she wouldn't lose it. God was going to give her the strength she needed *when* she needed it. I smiled at the dear man. "Here's your ticket," he said gently, handing me a train ticket.

The house shook! A train was going by the house! It felt more like an earthquake. We opened the door as the train whizzed passed only a few yards from us. The Lord and I ran and hopped onto the caboose as it went with great speed down the street in front of the Ten Boom's house. I clung to the bar on the caboose.

Suddenly, the train veered straight up fo the sky. It flew through the atmosphere and clouds. I hung on for dear life. I felt like I was going to fall off. At one point, my body was flung almost completely from the rails as it swerved and ran through the open air. In the chaos, I noticed the Lord, standing steadily, without support on the caboose. I yelled to Him, "How are you able to stand and not hang on like that?"

"Because I have faith," He replied calmly. With every ounce of faith I could muster, I started crawling my way towards Him. The train looped in the air and went up and down faster and faster. I finally made it to Him and clung on to Him. He was steady like the pole I had been hanging onto. But there was more there that I was hanging onto then just balance. I was hanging onto His faith.

I started enjoying myself. It felt like a carpet ride in space. A roller coaster of all roller coasters! I screamed out with glee. We laughed as it turned over and over and then came to a stop back on a street at on the city again. As we made our descend, He said to me slowly and carefully, "You are the love of My life."

As we got off, I noticed that the caboose was now the front of the train. I didn't see any other cars or an engine in sight. He stepped off and then held me by my waist as I jumped off. It had been a thrill. The Lord told me that the train represented my calling and I was going to have to have faith to stand. It was going to be an awesome ride. Now we were standing back in the city. We started walking down the dirt road. "Where are we going now?" I asked in excitement.

THE NURSERY

We stopped in front of a small building a lot like the Ten Boom house and Ezekiel's house. There was a large, open window in the front. The Lord boosted me up so that I could see in it. It was a house filled with toddlers. They all looked about three or four years in age. There must have been about twenty children in there with no sign of adult. They were playing so lovely together, laughing and having a wonderful time. There were two little ones on a teeter-totter I could see well. They did not notice me in the window. The Lord and I smiled at each other.

He opened the door to the little house. The children all looked up and screamed out almost with one accord, "Papa! Papa!" They all raced to Him and hugged Him. I loved seeing Him with them, He was so wonderful. There was a rainbow-colored rocking-chair in the far side of the room where there was a small fire. The house was a lot like the others I had seen inside.

Jesus sat down in the rocking chair while the children all sat down around Him in excitement. I sat down, unnoticed, in a rocking-chair on the other side of the room. Jesus began to tell a story. I honestly don't remember it, because I was so fascinated with Him, not the story. He basically acted out the whole thing. He was so vivid and expressive in His story telling and the children were absolutely captivated. *He never ceases to amaze me*, I thought. *Of course children adored Him.*

After His story, He stood up and looked at me. "Boys and girls, you may call her 'Mama'." He said, all the little eyes staring at me now.

They pivoted in their seats and mumbled quietly to themselves, "Mama... .mama..." I was wondering why He did this, when I heard a beautiful, wonderful sound. The sound of the children singing to Him. The closest I can describe it is a boy's choir. The harmonies were so intricate and beautiful. They sang:

"Sing a love that never ends..
She is Yours
And You are hers..."

At the end, Jesus picked up a small boy as he sang the last few words as a solo, "You are mine." But it felt like he was singing on behalf of me. His voice was so pure and high. Jesus kissed the little boy on the cheek and then we left.

"Who were those children, Lord? Were they human or angels?"

"They are the ones who have not been touched by the evils of this world. They have Heaven's blood in them."

"What does that mean, Lord?"

"They are the ones you will be working with. They will bring joy to the Earth."

"I don't understand, Lord, and I am desperate to understand."

"You will understand when you leave this place."

We walked a while longer and then stood together in front of a gigantic building. I recognized it immediately. The tabernacle!

CHAPTER 15

BACK TO THE TABERNACLE

W e started walking up the stairs. I stopped in the middle of the ascend. "What are you afraid of?" It seemed as if He had asked that question a lot of me lately.

"I am afraid that I will not accurately describe the tabernacle. There is so much about it in the Bible and I know so little about it."

"I have given you eyes to see. See."

We walked into the outer court area where I had seen Samuel so long ago. I saw the carvings on the gold walls of dogwood flowers and palm trees [61]. Samuel was still there, standing in the same place where I had left him with the Lord. They seemed as if they were just ghosts there as we walked passed the two figures. We entered a large room with pillars where I saw a small mat on the floor. *For Samuel*, I presumed. That's where he heard the Lord calling him when he was a little boy [62].

We walked passed a sacrificing table where I felt very heavy, like I was about to go into labor. I began asking the Lord for forgiveness from Him. I said that I was sorry that He had to die for me. We walked a little further where we came to a very thick, hanging curtain. It was like a black velvet, but it was very, very thick. It was torn down the center [63]. I knew exactly where we were. We walked through the veil.

Inside was a small room completely covered with a dark, green, silk material. It covered the floor, walls, and ceiling in one piece. It was not tightly draped against the walls, but almost casually hung with pleats all through it. In the middle of the room was a large stone table that looked a little like an ancient coffin. We walked up to it. "Take the lid off, woman," He said to me. I started heaving the lid off of the stone table. It was very heavy, but I was amazed to have the strength to do it. The lid slid off and fell to the floor with a massive *thud*.

Inside...inside...I couldn't believe it! Inside I could see the Arc of the Covenant! [64] It looked a little smaller than I thought it would be, but it was much more beautiful. From the top view of it, looking down into the stone cocoon around it, I could see the golden seraphim's wing spans. They were huge and seem to almost touch each other. It was all the most beautiful gold! I looked up at Jesus, wide-eyed. He looked down at the treasure.

"Mark My words, woman. When this resurfaces again, it will mark the prophecy that the Jews will be restored to Me. It will be right around the corner from the finding of this. Mark down the day and time you have seen it (March 17, 2007 at around 5:44 p.m.). I will restore My people again!"

I looked at Him, not knowing what He wanted to do next. I couldn't lift the thing, it was much to heavy and I didn't know how to grip it. I glanced away for a moment. In that one second, He took it out and sat it down on the stone table for full viewing. It was absolutely beautiful!

The Lord started perspiring. He seemed to be in some kind of stress. There were two horns I could see on each side of the Arc. I didn't think they were originally there. He grabbed hold of them and started to agonize in prayer. "Restore My people!" [65] He cried out to the Father. He began lamenting in intercession, still holding onto the horns. I stood there watching for a while, not knowing what to do. Sweat was dripping from Him and I started feeling the pain and longing to have whatever He wanted in prayer answered.

I walked over to Him. "If only I were a Jew. If only I were among Your people."

"Ah, but you are," He whispered, smiling a little, never losing His grip on the horns.

My heart reached out for Him in such distress, trying to make everything right. "I want to join in with You to pray whatever You want for Israel."

He surprised me by letting go of the Arc and throwing His arms around me. He was damp and hot and He kissed me repeatedly on my cheeks. He was elated for some reason because of what I just said. He hugged me again, rocking me a little side to side. "You have finally found what I made you for, My love. I have called you for this. I have asked you to pray My will be done and you have finally done it. I will lead you in intercession. Join in with Me in what I am praying for. Oh, My love, I love you! I love you!"

We held each other's hand, reaching to the Father's heart together. The power and anointing was beyond description as we boldly came. We pleaded out as one, "Forgive them, restore them, heal them, bring them!" Then, He let go of my hand in deep, deep pain of Spirit. He grabbed hold of the horns once again and ROARED like a lion. [66] Under the power of it, I felt my body totally collapse.

I opened my eyes, on the floor beside the Arc. Jesus was sitting against the stone table right next to me. He looked a little tired and overheated. I picked my head up and asked, "Oh, no, did I fall asleep? I'm so sorry, Lord. Why are you not praying?"

He looked at me with a smile, "You did not fall asleep, you were knocked out. I am just waiting here for the Father to answer our prayer."

THE BEAUTIFUL PLACE

We finally stood up slowly and walked to the wall on the other side of the doorway we had come in. Jesus moved back the silk fabric like it was a curtain. A beautiful place appeared. It was beyond words. We stepped into a beautiful meadow, knee deep in flowers. There was a waterfall that was pouring into a pool. I asked, "How many waterfalls are in the city, Lord?"

"As many as there need be," He answered. It was always a place of refreshment for me. I could see a little bunny rabbit working it's way though the flowers. It was warm and breezy. I decided to pick some flowers. When I picked the first one, I heard the Spirit sing, "I love you." The next one sang the same thing in a different tone. I picked a handful. As I did, the Spirit sang with each one, "I love you... I love you... I love you..." It was like a chorus singing a harmony of "I love you's" for me.

I ran through the flowers, listening to the "I love you's" sing to me as I ran past. The wind was even singing softly as it sprinted passed me. Everything seemed to be alive with the Spirit's love for me! Everything was singing. It was beyond joy.

I dived in the water, splashing Jesus as I went in. I offered for Him to come in, too. But He just lay in the grass, sucking on a flower stem, His arms under His head. "I don't need it," He said to me. I sure did. I splashed Him some more. He finally stood up, trying to block Himself from the splashing as we giggled. I ran to Him, giving Him a big, wet hug. He protested meekly and I laughed at Him. *Pay back!*

A female angel appeared. She was a small, Asian woman that looked middle-aged. A tent appeared behind her. "My dear, it is time to get dressed."

"Just a little more time..." I pleaded. It was strange that up until that time I had hurried my time away with the Lord. There was such a pull on my heart to get back to Earth all the time. I felt like I needed to tell what happened to me as quickly as possible. One last hug and I was in the tent.

She started taking off my wet outer garments when Pat suddenly appeared in front of me. She looked like she was see-through. Her eyes were closed as if in prayer. "Amy, you must come back immediately. I have something I have to tell you."

(I opened my eyes in my bedroom on Earth. I moaned and turned over, my body aching from the sudden departure. I phoned Pat. This is what she prophesied to me:

"I am pouring out my joy on you as you have never known. It is important for you to bring this back to the Body. They need it so! They need to know that I am not a task master or slave driver. They need to know that I am not burdensome. They need to know that I am a light yoke. [67]")

THE REVELATION

I was brought back to the tent a day later. I was completely dressed in a beautiful, pink gown with tapestry embroidery on it. It was my ball gown. I came out of the tent to greet Him in the beautiful place. I walked towards Him. "I must

have very little faith for you to have to show me all of this."
I said smiling.

He looked at me intently and then brushed His finger on
my jaw line and said, "I love the weak things." Butterflies
overtook me from head to toe. I laughed, trying not to
swallow any. Just when I had enough of the fluttering all
over me, the Lord waved His hand and they flew away.

"They're so beautiful! Why did you give butterflies such
a short life after they turn into butterflies?"

"Butterflies represent resurrection. I was not with you
(meaning mankind) long after the resurrection."

A sudden burst of revelation hit me seemingly out of no
where! I got the revelation (or at least one of the revelations) to
Ezekiel's wheel in a wheel he saw. I held my breath and then
let it out exuberantly exclaiming, "I have to go tell Ezekiel!" I
ran out of the park towards the curtains of the Holy of Holies.
I only got two steps into the door, the Lord starting to follow
behind me, when I fell to the floor by the Arc. I felt a heavi-
ness in my abdomen, a pressure. I felt myself almost faint.
I do not know if I was there hours or minutes, but all of a
sudden it lifted and I got up running as before.

I ran through the Tabernacle, through the pillars on the
porch. I ran out to the road and stopped. I had no idea how
to get to Ezekiel's house. I knew it was on the other side of
the city, and I could probably find it if I had a couple of hours,
but I needed to see him immediately. The Lord strolled out
teasingly– He knew I would need Him. He hailed a gold
carriage with an angel on a bike, peddling it instead of a horse
pulling it. We climbed on and it went *shwoosh*. I thought it
was going to be a rocky ride, but it was very smooth.

In just less than a minute, I was knocking on the door
to Ezekiel's house. In fact, I was *pounding* on it. Ezekiel
opened the door. I threw myself in an embrace on the little
man and then tried to compose myself as I gleefully tried to
report my findings. I could smell fresh bread baking inside.

"The outer wheel..." I said, trying to catch my breath, "is the Word coming from Heaven to Earth. The smaller one inside is the praises and intercessions made by the saints going back to Heaven."

He looked at me calmly and smiled. "He just told me the same thing."

CHAPTER 16

THE BRIGHT AND MORNING STAR

We rode back slowly to the Tabernacle. I bent my head back against the seat to relax a little. I was tired. I walked up the steps to the Tabernacle, the Lord falling slowly behind. I couldn't look at Him. My mind was actually tired of the revelations I received from His beautiful face.

"Look upon Me," He said gently and forcefully at the same time. I just couldn't. He came up behind me, a step behind, and put His mouth on my right shoulder, holding my right hand. Looking through the pillars, where the inside of the tabernacle had been, I could see the sun rising. I could not see anything but the sun through those pillars. It was brilliant and gold as if the sun was right there where I could touch it. I turned my face away, blinded by the radiance.

"Look upon Me!" A voice called from inside the sun. I looked directly into the sun. There I saw Jesus- the same one still holding my hand- but the *King* Jesus, arrayed in an emerald robe as if He was coming out of a stain glass window.

"I am your Bright and Morning Star!"[68] He proclaimed. I could feel a hand on my back keeping me from flying down the steps and possibly across the street, so great was the impact of the sight!

I knelt down to my knees. The Jesus that was standing next to me was no more. He was just the Bright and Morning Star in front of me. He looked at me so sternly that I almost didn't recognize Him. "What do you want from Me?" He asked with His majestic voice.

"I want to kiss you," was my surprising answer. There was so much to the statement that I had just said. I didn't want anything from Him. Just to show my affections toward Him. His face changed in expression. He looked down at the ground and then back to me. He seemed to be moved and a little shy. It seemed like such an odd thing to feel as He stood there, arrayed in His glory.

I stood up. Huge, gorgeous, gold wings appeared on my back. I walked towards Him with no fear. I knew Him, this King in splendor! I slowly kissed His beautiful beard once. I was so close to Him that His radiant light and glory seemed to be mine as well to anyone that could look on. I was sharing it with Him!

THE BALCONY

He motioned me out to the left of the porch at the Tabernacle. We walked out onto a beautiful balcony that hadn't been there before. Below us were thousands upon thousands of angels, both women and men. We were like the royalty one sees rarely, stepping out of their palace to wave to their subjects. They were all crying and screaming with joy!

I could hear my story being told to each of them as a song that had been sung here long ago. They knew my story even better than we would know a story of a famous hero like King Arthur. They knew it all, the whole awful truth. I could hear the story being sung around campfires long ago and told in homes of angels of yesterday. They were singing,

"The one who crucified Him,
The one who nailed Him to the tree.
The one who beat Him,
Stripped Him,
The one who brought *all* suffering on Him-
She is the Queen.
She is the one He chooses to love
for all eternity!
She is the one He shows His glory with!
She has become *one* with the Bright and Morning Star!"

And their cries were that of the revelation of the deep love of their God who would dare do this! They were crying and cheering for Him and for our love. We stood there, close together, holding each other's hands like we were going to dance. He was holding my right hand by His left. He stretched it out high and brave like a crescendo to a song. It was like the referee holding the champion's hand up. They roared with excitement.

We each had a beautiful crown on. Mine was silver and diamonds and His was gold with jewels. I took my crown off and threw it down to the ground where His feet were. Another one appeared on my head. I did it again. Still another one appeared on my head. It became a very natural motion that I didn't grow tired of.[69]

Finally, He lowered my arm and walked me back the direction we had come out from. We were not on the steps of the Temple, though. We were inside an ancient palace. The pillars were like you would see in a Bible movie. We sat on a padded bench where I asked a question that was even more bold than the last.

"Show me Your stripes," I asked quietly. It was not out of doubt or even interest, I wanted to see these scars because they were a part of Him. They were the part that gave life to me. He was wearing a two piece garment that changed colors every time He took a step. Right then it was a red color. He had a robe-like top that tied at the waist and a skirt-like bottom that had gathers at the waist.

He took off the shirt-like robe to His waist and turned around. I wasn't sure that these scars would even be there because they are never mentioned after the resurrection as being so. But there they were. They stretched down and around Him and even onto His arms. They were not fine-lines of stripes. They were deformed-looking, large-width scars. They raised out of His back like pink ribbons. There was not an inch of skin left untouched.

I started hyperventilating. I left Him there, not being able to stand the emotion any longer. I ran to the right of the beautiful room where I found stairs much like the ones that led out of the bath house. I had on a beautiful white dress with purple material that tied to my arms and hung. The purple material picked up weightlessly as I ran down the stairs. The stairs turned like the ones out of the bath house into a living area- just like the bath house. This *was* the bath house! I put my hand on the left of the doorway and cried.

I could feel Him coming.

He put His hands on my shoulders as they quivered in sorrow. "It's finished."[70] I turned around and looked at His face.

"But it's not finished, is it? Every time I sin, you can feel it again."

"Every time *you* sin? Never! It's just a little sting when it's you...You love Me." He wiped the tears from my eyes with His thumb. [71]

142

I opened the door to the living area of the bath house that went out onto the street. I stepped out with the Lord. I wondered how we had gotten here, but there were already so many mysterious thing about this place... I looked to the left that went to the bus station (home). I looked to the right which lead out of the City (also to home). I then looked straight ahead. Straight ahead was the park and then beyond that the streets that would take me to David and Corie to the left and Ezekiel on the right.

I fought the temptation to run back to where David was and asked the Lord, "Where do you want me to go? Lord, you know exactly who I need to see."

"Walk where you feel to walk and it will lead you to the right direction," He said. He seemed to trust me. It wasn't a hard decision. I wanted to stay in the City, so I walked straight, passed the park. In fact, I walked a little into the park, just to see the beautiful tents that had greeted me here. I walked up the little hill and looked through the trees to the tents. They were cream-colored and beautiful, waving in the breeze. There was a small crowd of people gathered around and in them. Even before I was finished here, I marveled, they are already following in my footsteps. I was pleased with this. I sighed. The more of the Body here, the better.

WHOM JESUS LOVED

I walked out of the park and stepped onto the road. There was a small house that sat across the street from the park. Funny, I had not noticed it before. It was much like the other houses, but I didn't have much time to ponder this. I didn't even have time to knock or even step near the door. John came bounding out! How I knew Him, I cannot tell you, but I instantly recognized him as I would recognize my own brother. He embraced me and we kissed each other's cheeks emotionally and solemnly.

He then put his forehead to my forehead and cupped his hands around my jaw bone. A wave of love so deep, it was unbelievably painful, surged in me. This was an impartation of the disciple whom Jesus loved! [72] How long it lasted, I cannot tell you. But every ounce of that love was directed to humankind and the Lord. I thought I was going to die, it was so heavy.

"You have come here to me, and to all of the ones you have come to here because you wanted to. You chose each of us. And by the looks of who you have chosen, you want to suffer as we have." He smiled. "He has captivated you, too, has He? You will suffer, my dear," he prophesied, "so that your backs will match."

He then looked at Jesus. With tears and desperation in his face, still holding onto me he cried, "Oh that I could have died for You! That would have been the greatest honor of all!"[73]

Jesus rushed to him to quiet him, "You *lived* for Me!" They held unto each other, sobbing.

I could hear the muffled cries of John, "If only I could have suffered more for your name!"[74]

The Holy Spirit whispered to me, "What you are witnessing is actually happening at this moment in Heaven."

John finally let go and brought us into the house where there was a huge fire in the middle of the room, blazing. There was no smoke, however. A few tree limbs kept it going without burning them up. John rushed to the Lord as soon as the door was closed and hugged Him close. He put his forehead on His chest. Jesus held Him tightly and kissed him on his dark head.

John had a young look about him, like a movie star that hadn't ever stopped looking like a teenager. It didn't seem strange at all of the spectacle they were making of themselves. John finally left the Master and held onto me to impart in me again. The surge went deep, but felt more numb this time. Jesus came over to the two of us and put his arms around us as we worked.

When everyone was relaxing later, I sat next to John and put my hand on his large hand resting on his knee. "I don't want to suffer," I said quietly and meekly. I didn't want the Lord to hear me.

"You are *afraid* of suffering. Almost everyone is. It's okay, my dear." He was so gentle. I got up to walk toward the Lord. John called back to me softy, "Beloved," He said. I stopped, not turning. "Remember who you are."

I walked back over to the Lord. The atmosphere quickly turned joyous when I went up to Him. He lifted me up by my legs. I flew into the air as he turned us round and round. I laughed heartily. I needed it.

THE ISLAND

The house started flashing like lightening around me. The Lord put me down as I watched in awe. At some seconds it looked like walls surrounded us, and then it would magically open up to a beach scene. The walls eventually started vanishing to reveal the beach around us. Small shrubs, no large trees that I could see, were along the dunes. A small, sandy beach was surrounded by water. It was not turquoise, it almost looked dirty. There didn't seem to be any shade on the island.

The Island of Patmos.[75] This is where he had his vision of Revelation. This is where he was exiled and forced to do hard labor– after being boiled in oil.

The three of us climbed a sand dune together. A plateau held a couple of dozen people on it. I was shocked by this, because I thought we were alone. The people, both men and women, were working very hard and did not stop or even look up as we approached. They each had a different kind of tool in their hands, but it looked like they were each trying to achieve a common, individual goal. "What are they doing?" I asked.

"They are digging their own wells," John replied softly. "Each is trying to get to water by a different means. That one is trying through vanity to reach the water. That one is trying through prosperity of money... What they don't understand is that *He* is a well that never runs dry." It was a sad sight. Some of them would cry out and try to drink the little bits of water they would pull up after working and working. They would then spit it out because it was salt water.

The worst was one of them pulling up a large, wet chunk of dung and trying to get refreshed from it. I turned my head away as that one collapsed in agony. Still another, an old man, had worked his entire life for a little sip and received absolutely nothing at all. He died in front of my eyes.

"These are no representations," The Lord replied solemnly. "These are actual people on Earth that you are seeing."

I sprang into action! I shouted at them to look at me and listen to me. They never even looked at me. I went into their faces and pleaded with them. "Here! Here! Here He is, the well that never runs dry! The Living Water walks right there!" But none of them, not one, even looked up. At one point, John brought me to a lady who was very close to the edge of the mound. This was actually a good thing. One more inch and she could fall into the arms of the anointing of the Lord that resided on the shore.

"She is digging for water with her love for her family and friends. She is very close to the truth!" John said to me, leading me towards her.

"My dear lady..." I said tenderly. There was no response. "My dear lady!" I said loudly. I crouched down, nose to nose with her. When there was still no response, "My dear lady! You are so close! You cannot be fulfilled with any love on this Earth! He is the only Way!" She batted me away like a mosquito. But a hopeful thought crossed my mind– she had heard me!

"I refuse to believe there is something wrong with my family!" She said sternly back to me. I was shocked.

CHAPTER 17

THE BOAT

I walked back to the Lord and John wearily to get some advice. Before I could ask for their comments, I looked up and behind them, a ship was coming. I motioned for them to look. They knew it was coming. We all walked back down to the shore where it was speedily approaching.

"Is this a good thing or a bad thing?" I asked the Lord, not taking my eyes off the boat.

"A good thing for you. A very good thing for you."

As the ship got closer. It looked like an old ship that the pilgrims had come in. It had a bow that went straight up and formed a cross. The ship was wooden and you could see it had never been painted. It pulled up on shore and slid to a halt. *How odd*, I though, *they have no fear of getting stuck here.*

Out of the ship came a dear friend who is an intercessor at my church. She looked very young and carried a large sword on her belt. "We've come to take you to your place in ministry." She smiled. She looked like the pictures of Joan of Arc I had seen. I climbed aboard unresistantly. The Lord and John vanished.

The ship was clean and beautiful. "I'll show you your quarters," she said with a smile. A small hutch-like room was at the back of the ship. When I entered, it was just a small room, not even able to let me lie down in. It had a simple bench on three sides with white, satin padding. It was very pretty, but seemed almost inadequate for a long journey.

"Where is everyone else staying?" I asked, somehow knowing this was a ship filled with people.

"Oh, I'll show 'ya. They're down below in the intercessory floor." She walked towards the middle of the ship where she pulled up a door in the floor. We went down the ladder to the galley. Large, swaying beds hung bunk bed style from the ceiling. They were each dressed with extremely comfortable looking satin comforters and pillows. They each had a little bed skirt that swayed to and fro. Each bed was done up with orange and purple satin. One had an orange comforter and purple pillows and skirt, the next had a purple comforter with orange bed skirt and pillows.

I stood there in awe of the display. This was no pirate ship. "Let me take turns so that they can have the upstairs quarters sometimes as well." I felt guilty that I was going to have such a private place to go.

"There is a reason you are separated," she replied.

Something started to feel funny. I looked up and around at the floors. The walls, ceiling and floors were dark wood and a little dirty. From the ceiling hung a huge clue. Shackles. " I don't think you got everything when you cleaned this place out."

"Why? What's the matter?"

"This use to be a slave ship– the spirit of which still resides here. These intercessors are being enslaved."

"By whom?" She asked in horror.

"By a spirit of slavery. Let's all pray in the Spirit." Women appeared in all corners of the ship. They all prayed in tongues in a very high pitch for just a few minutes. The spirit that had bound them by desperate pastors needing their anointing was leaving. The spirit that had bound them by their own religious thought was being loosened. The curses over their lives that had enslaved them were being cut off. Freedom was being birthed there.

As their voices rang up, the walls, floors and ceilings were being supernaturally draped in a white satin material. The shackles disappeared. I climbed up the ladder. As I did, the wooden ship started turning white! It was like someone spilled a huge pot of white paint– it was spreading every-where. Then, they stopped abruptly.

I suddenly stopped cold. "Where's Sean?" I hadn't seen my husband in the city since the first night, and yet I found it absolutely imperative that he be on this ship.

"He didn't come aboard, Amy," one of them said. I looked desperately around. "He's on the island!" How I knew, I do not know, but I did.

"Give me a life boat!" They looked at me, blinking. "NOW!" I yelled. They scurried around and lowered me down.

As they did, one of them called down, "We can't slow down for you, they'll be no way you'll be able to catch up to us."

"My husband is stronger than you think!" I yelled back, confident that he could row the boat faster than the ship was sailing. I rowed with all my strength back to the island. I saw the Lord and John standing in the same place I had left them.

"Where is he?" I asked breathlessly. They pointed me in the direction towards the left and followed me as I ran. I found him immediately. He was playing solemnly with our two children by the shore. A spirit of worthlessness was around him. "Sean!" He didn't look up. "Sean, I need you, this instant!" The worthlessness vanished off of him and he sprang to his feet.

He gathered the two kids in his arms and ran back to where the life boat was. We got in and I held onto the little ones while he rowed with great speed and strength. We caught up to the boat. Then the thought occurred to me: How were we going to get on? As I was thinking this thought, the four of us were lifted out of our boat by an awesome, unseen hand and placed on the ship. The intercessors gathered around us with joy like we were a new baby just born.

Life onboard the ship for the day was beautiful. The weather could not have been more gorgeous. I stood on top of my cabin, holding onto a pole on the ship. I watched behind me while the children played with Sean and the others happily. I thought of getting them life preservers to wear, but then remembered where I was. I thought it wasn't very productive of me.

I turned back to the ocean racing around us. I had a small telescope in my hands and I was watching for land. I was in agony. I couldn't stand being without the Lord. My heart ached and moaned. I hadn't even said good-bye to Him. I had just assumed that He would come with me. I'm sure the Holy Spirit had, but I loved that Jesus was flesh and bone like me.

"Captain," a small voice was calling someone. "Captain..." the voice continued from behind me. "Amy!" the voice finally shouted at me. I finally turned around.

"Were you trying to call me?"

"Yes," the young, red-headed woman said in relief. "What do you see?"

I looked again. I could see land! "I see an island!" It was approaching dead ahead. I saw tall palm trees. "Stop and anchor the boat!"

THE BEAUTIFUL ISLAND

"What should we do, Captain?" someone asked.

"The Lord would not put it in our path for us to just ignore," another said.

"It could be a trap," yet another said.

"We should inquire of the Lord," I said authoritatively. The ship stopped and every hand was on deck praying on her knees. After a short time, I looked up to where the island was. There was a light coming from it and in it, yes, in the light was a *person*! *The* Person! "The Lord is on the island!" I sang out. Without even thinking, I jumped off the ship. I screamed a little on the way down because it was a very long way down.

I heard someone call out, "You'll never make it! Wait for the lifeboats to be put in! It's a mile away!"

But it didn't matter how far it was. I swam and swam in the cold, turquoise ocean towards the shore. It seemed like only a few feet, so great was my desire to see Him. I plodded out of the water at shore, sopping wet, and embraced the King. After a while of affectionate little kisses and hug after hug, I asked, "Why did you leave me?" I knew He did not, but I didn't really know how else to ask such a thing.

"I wanted you to miss Me," He teased.

"Will you come with me this time on the ship?"

"I will, but you will not see Me. I am a bit of a distraction for you." He smiled broadly. "It seems all you want to do when you see Me is shower affection on Me and there is much work to be done on that ship."

The boats started coming up on shore and the intercessors started getting out and stretching their land legs. He motioned for me to come with Him. We started digging where He told me to. We pulled up a heavy treasure chest. [77] It flung open upon impact on the beach and showed it's gold and jewels to everyone. We did this again and again, until there were seven treasure chests laying all in a vertical row. I tried to work as fast as possible. I could work about fifty times faster here it seemed. The Lord finally stopped me and said, "Do not try to speed up your time with Me, even if it is hard work."

The Lord motioned for the intercessors to go and take whatever they wanted from the treasure chests. Some of them just stood there and watched the others plowing through, treasure chests left untouched still. The Lord and I had to physically bring them over to the chests to pick out what they wanted, so great was their feeling of unworthiness. "Some need a divine word from Me, even about things I have already told them were theirs for the taking," He remarked.

"And what of you, Beloved?" He asked. I stood there with Him alone while the others were ooh-ing and awe-ing over the treasure chests. I looked up into His eyes. He pulled a gold chain from His sleeve. It was a necklace of sorts with a purple stone the size of my fist attached to it. He opened it. There was a clock inside. On the other side, I saw a picture of His face. He was laughing in the picture. Then, the picture started becoming clouded with a red film that flooded that side of the pendant. I touched it. It was thick blood. "My timing," He said.

"The kids!" I said to Him, remembering they needed to see Him, too. I ran over and got my two children and brought them over to Him. He knelt down, each of them sitting on a different knee of His. He made a little train appear in the air above Christian and then made it disappear just as quickly. Christian was overjoyed! He loved trains. Cora looked at Him, beaming, seemingly expecting something. He looked at her, too, smiling. Then, He grabbed hold of her and started tickling her. She shrieked with laughter.

"Sean!" I yelled a few yards away. Sean stood there, waiting for an invitation from the Lord. Funny how I never waited for an invitation. The kids clung to His legs as He held out His arms to Sean. Sean walked strongly to Him and embraced Him. He kissed him on his cheek and held him again. "You have exactly what it takes to deal with all of this, Sean. The Holy Spirit will help you with her. She's a handful, that one." The Lord looked at me and winked, still holding onto Sean.

They didn't seem to want to let go. "You know, you are more to Me than just her husband." The Lord was talking quietly to Him. He paused for impact and almost to gather His own emotions. "You are one of my greatest friends. One of my best friends." Sean let go and nodded his head quietly, not looking at the Lord as he pulled away.

The people started getting in the boats to leave. I walked back to the Lord for some final instructions. "What do we have to eat?" I asked. I was concerned about the amount of supplies aboard.

"You know that here, you only need to eat when you need to eat," He remarked. It was true about sleeping as well. I nodded somehow understanding.

I started walking back with my hands behind my back. Suddenly, I could feel a very small treasure chest in my hands behind my back. I heard Him say, "Teach them how to love Me."

I turned around, the treasure chest disappearing. "It would be my greatest honor!" I ran back to Him and threw my arms around Him. I held Him and held Him. I finally walked down to the turquoise water. I did not get in a little boat. I splashed into the water! I got back in and fell in again. I started laughing and inviting the children and Sean in. The kids ran in, splashing unabashed.

Sean stood by the Lord who said, "She's playing... that's good." Sean nodded in approval. It was a rare sight. The Lord and Sean joined us, splashing and jumping in and out of the water. The Lord catapulted Christian and Cora out of the water and they jumped back in, laughing and screaming. We had a marvelous time, playing there.

It was finally time to get back into the little boat toward the ship. I was the last one in. He called back to me, not wanting, it seemed, for me to go, either. "You will be sore from that swim from the boat to Me."

I showed my back to Him, pulling my dress shoulders down a little. "Until I have a back that matches Yours, I'll keep going."

"Amy..." I walked back to Him again. "You might not be able to see those stripes on your back, My love. They maybe only internal." He seemed to be warning me, having me count the cost.

"Are you the Healer?" I asked.[78]

"Yes."

"Are You the Comforter?"[79]

"Yes."

"Then, I think I am in good hands," I said and walked away. I sat at the side of the little boat and kept eye contact with the Lord until He became smaller and smaller. I sang, "I love You, I love You, I love You," over and over again in my head to Him.

BACK ONBOARD

The little boat was hoisted aboard with ropes that anchored to the sides. They were already asking questions, "Where to now, Captain?" I hated that they called me that. "Are we going to inquire of the Lord again?"

"I will," I said, wanting some space from the crew. I went into my little, white cabin and got on my knees. "Where do we go from here, Lord?" I asked. I waited.

The reply was, "You already know what direction your heart is pointed towards."

I came out abruptly from my cabin after only a few minutes. "North, north-east," I said. What was I doing? *I've never even been on a boat like this, let alone be in charge of it.* We sailed along on the beautiful seas. I called out, "Who is called to do cleaning?"

"I am."

"I am," two scruffy looking women replied. Cleaning duty is what I was always called to when ministering, so I knew their hearts. They were the ones that ached for all things to be pure. I nodded and they started. A few of them helped shake out the beds and scrub down the walls. They were getting tired, so a darkness fell and rain came spattering down for only a few minutes to wash the outside of the ship clean again. When everything started moving like clock work again, something happened.

CHAPTER 18

THE LEVIATHAN

There was a huge jolt and the boat stopped, as if stopped by *something*. An enormous rock was protruding out of the water, in the middle of the open seas. It was very peculiar that we did not see it. What was most peculiar is that it was even there at all. Everyone ran all over the place. I was holding onto the mast, so I clung to it so that I wouldn't fall.

Just as we were gaining our composure again, out of the water emerged a horrible beast! It was similar in looks to a dragon, but not exactly. It seemed to have a white slime on it's green, reptile-like scales. It's ears flew open like wings.

"Get down below! Now!" I called out to everyone. They all obeyed immediately, so great was the terror of what we were seeing. The last person down was Sean. I could hear him talking as he started to close the galley door.

"The captain said everyone get down here!" One of them yelled to him.

"I'm not with you, I'm with her!" He yelled back and came out of the galley to stand on the deck with me. He had gone down there to get a huge sword, bigger than even he was as a six foot, broad-shoulder man. He had my sword, it's animal covering worn and peeling. He stood at the bow and got close to the monster.

"This boat is surrounded by angels, this battle is not ours..." I started to say. But Sean had a different idea, he swung the sword with all his might.

"Sean, no!" I screamed. But it was too late. The beast's neck was cut apart and his head fell into the ocean. Sean rushed back to me.

"Why did you try to stop me?"

"I wanted to talk to it!" I yelled back to him.

"Talk to it?" He said, his face a blazing red, "Amy, you don't talk to these things, you kill them."

"I needed information out of him!"

"Information? What are you talking about?"

"I needed to know it's name!" I screamed in his face. People started emerging from the galley and cautiously looking around. Sean just stood there, watching me walk away, breathing heavily. "Who's called as the dis-lodger?" I asked the mass of people.

"I am, I'll get us off the blasted rock!" I was a little amazed to see another man on the ship.

"And who is the inspector?" I yelled out. A young woman stood before me. "Take a team down there and find out what our damage is."[80]

"Already done," she replied. "There is no damage. It must have been a smooth rock."

"Don't count on it," I said, knowing the strength of the ship we were on. I walked away and slammed the door to my quarters.

The Lord's voice started immediately and almost frantically, "This is not the end! There's more of them! Gird yourself. I have placed that rock for you to stumble on so that you can take care of this thing. And Sean has done you a great service by dealing with the worst of this pride. He is your protector, Amy. You must heed his advice on matters as if you hired him as your expert on security. I have hired him."

I punched the wall in my cabin. He continued sternly, "This is the place where your flesh will die. You will leave your body on this boat and walk out of it a new being."

"Kill my flesh, Lord," I said. All of a sudden, I felt a huge bump. I breathed a sigh because I thought we were dislodged. I threw back the door to discover utter panic instead. We were still stuck on that rock, but the monster had emerged again. It had six heads! We had only seen the one huge head. The other five were only a few feet from our ship, smaller, but looking exactly like the large one. Everyone else was screaming and running for safety. I did not have to tell them to get down below. Sean stayed with me, though, much to my chagrin. This time he let me do it my way, though.

"You killed our mother!" The five heads shrieked and hissed in agony.

"Yes, and I will kill you, too, if you do not tell me what I ask you." Their heads waved around like they were dizzy from the pain. "Who are you?"

"You know who we are, we are Pride!"

"And who on this ship has allowed you to come near us!" I demanded.

"*You* have summoned us, *Captain*," they sneered. I stood there for a second trying to take it in.

"Oh, God, how do I deal with this?" I whispered in desperation. I started walking towards the heads. I started speaking to them, "He did not choose me as captain because I had something He needed. He choose me because I had nothing. He chose the weakest one here to show off His strength." They were silent. I did not know what to make of it.

I had an idea. I grabbed hold of Sean's hand and sat him down. I grabbed a bowl that was on the deck and rushed back over to him, filling it up with water on the way. I ignored the monster and started washing his feet. "I give up my rights to this ship as captain to you," I said.

"No," He whispered back to me. We felt a breeze and looked up. The monster was gone. I staggered back to my room. After a few moments, Sean came in. "I will keep this from the crew," he said quietly.

"Are they all on deck?" I asked, brushing my hair back. He nodded. I walked out. "I need everyone's attention.... What just happened here was God putting a stumbling block in my way so that I could deal with my own demon of pride. It was my fault that this ship was in jeopardy. I want to be straight with you all, the Lord has told me this will not be the last time. You can leave through the lifeboats if you feel you do not want to deal with these things with me. I will understand." I waited for the response patiently.

"We have been chosen to help you reach your destination," one said bravely. "We will not leave you." I nodded and went back in my cabin.

THE ASSIGNMENTS

More than a day later, I finally woke up in my little cabin, my legs hunched together uncomfortably because I couldn't fully recline. It was hot and the little window was bringing in fresh streams of hot light every second onto me. I opened the door. A beautiful breeze nearly knocked me off my feet. It felt so good. I was sweaty and my head was spinning. I stumbled out. *This must be what it feels like to have a hangover,* I thought to myself.

On deck, Sean was answering questions and everyone was busy, although it seemed a bit disorganized, yet functioning. I went over towards him, holding my forehead with my hand, wincing from the light. "How are the kids?"

"They're fine," he replied. I was trying to sense any kind of anger in his voice for me shrugging off duties so long in my cabin. But, at that moment, I didn't care enough to dissect his tone. "They're down below playing. They're having a great time." I staggered away.

"Too many people", I said to myself. "I've gotta get away from all of it."

Someone, to my embarrassment, must have overheard me because a young woman's voice replied, "There's a seat up there on the mast." I nodded and started climbing the mast. I had changed sometime in the passed day, because I was wearing a beautiful, silk sun dress. It was in a tie-dye pattern in red that tied at the neck.

"Not exactly what a captain of a ship would wear," I remarked to myself as I climbed. When I reached the top, watching the footing with a long dress on, I noticed there was a bucket-like area to sit in. It was pretty comfortable. Only my head was visible so my body was protected from the harsh wind conditions. My ears weren't though, so I couldn't hear anything but the wind. That was really fine. I didn't really care what was going on below anyway. I had braced myself for another rock and another monster, but it hadn't come yet.

The view was magnificent. Blue sky, blue ocean.... Holy Spirit...

"Get yourself down from here!" The Holy Spirit said sternly. "I have put you in charge of this ship, man your people! Teach your people. Get them together now." I sighed and gathered myself another moment. That was not allowed either, "Go now!" He said again. I grumbled a little and started making my descent.

"Gather everyone on the deck," I said to Sean. He knowingly did not include the children and gave them free reign down below to play by themselves. Dozens of people gathered immediately. They all sat down on the floor and awaited for me to begin. A podium was brought to me and I asked a teenager aboard if he would bring me the Word. He went back in my cabin and emerged immediately. The pages flipped in the wind when I lay it on the podium.

"What do you want me to teach, Lord?" And there we waited for Him. It came within a few minutes, a beautiful, light anointing. "Thank you, Lord, for this new anointing. We are not heavy any longer. Your yoke is light around our necks. Holy Spirit, You are our light, You are our ocean, You are our ship, You are our air. Thank You that You light our way. Thank You that You hold us up and keep us afloat. Thank you that You are the vehicle that takes us where You want us to go. But thank You most of all that You are the very air we breathe. You are the only thing keeping us alive."

I paused again, waiting for instructions from Him. "He wants me to lay hands on all of you and tell you what your jobs are here on this boat." Some of them cleared out, already been called to their specific jobs.

I went over to the first person. "You are the one who will catch us fish to eat." She nodded excitedly. Sean prepared the nets for her.[81]

The second person, "You are the one who will man the wheel and rudders." She nodded and took her position.[82]

Next, "You are the one who will be in charge of the dishes." I didn't really understand that one, but she was excited about it. Sean had a large crate brought to her on ropes. It was filled with white dishes. She was also given a set of paintbrushes to paint each plate and was given orders by Sean that she was also in charge of setting the tables and the ambiance of the meals. She would create a setting in which people would want to eat.[83]

The next young woman bowed her head as I touched her. I couldn't give her anything to do and that greatly annoyed me. "The Lord says your only job here is to make yourself holy." She didn't look up.

The next person was a dear man I knew, "You are in charge of the beauty of this ship. You will make sure that this ship is always beautiful. You will also make sure that all of us are dressed and looking very beautiful every day. This is done because we will not know when a passenger will be supernaturally placed on this boat. We also never know when we will come to another island. We must always be ready to be attractive to the lost." [84]

I stopped. I needed refueling. I took a few steps away and then felt water splash onto my head. It was cool and refreshing and I felt like I was in love again. I went back to start on the person behind him, but the Holy Spirit corrected me and I went all the way to the other side of the line.

It was a person I didn't like. I asked the Lord to forgive me for having prejudice and not loving her and asked Him to give me the job she was to do. "You will be the cleaner of the Captain's cabin. Every time I go out of there, you will go in and clean it, paying close attention to any dust. Any flesh you see lying there on the floor, do not be alarmed, the Lord has regenerated my parts. Discard them with a small broom and dust pan. You will be the one keeping me in line." [85] *No wonder I don't like her*, I thought.

Next woman, "You are in charge of scraping the barnacles off the ship when the anchor is down. [86] The Lord says for you not to feel alarmed because the laws of nature are different here and you will not drown. I thought you were going to have to have scuba gear..." I laughed. "He also says not to be overwhelmed because one or two barnacles a month form and you can easily get them if you keep it up."

I started to go on to the next person, but I couldn't. "He says you have another job. You are in charge of making sure the galley is clean. You are also to never to go onto the islands. He wants you to stay aboard the ship until it makes port. You will be in charge of the security while we are ashore. You may have to fight some demons off while we are gone. Hold them at bay until I can come in with rein-forcements." She nodded happily. I shook my head. They each seemed to really love their jobs.

[87]Next person was a man I had not yet seen on the ship. He seemed to look like a different nationality. He had an oriental appearance, but his face was slightly larger on one side than the other. I lay my hands on him and heard very clearly, "Murder." I was astonished and quickly removed my hands. I asked the Lord to take out anything in me that was causing this and tried again. Before I lay my hands on him again, he kissed my left knee very delicately and said, "I am your helper. I am loving you. I will help you." I nodded, trying to be polite and put my hands on his head again. "Murder, murder, murder, murder, murder." It was a voice saying it over and over again very quickly. He looked up at me, smiling, not realizing what I had heard. I looked over besides him.

A tall, heavy boned, young woman was the only one left to give a job to after him. I whispered to her, "Go wait for me in the captain's quarters." She happily took off. I was not going to allow anything to jeopardize her receiving from the Lord.

"Who are you?" I asked the strange person sternly. Then, he knew I knew. His flesh pulled off him like a bloody banana peel and his real self emerged. He was a lizard like, naked thing that had that same white film on him the dragon did. He was hairless with big eyes and a big mouth. He looked alien. He stood up and looked me in the eye.

"Gag him!" I yelled. Sean and two other intercessors came over with long sticks with wire on the end like a dog catcher would use. They pulled them tight around his neck. "Now you listen to me," I said to the demon. "In Jesus name, you are not allowed to say anything against my Lord! You are only to answer my questions, nothing more! Do you understand?" I hated blasphemy and had enough of it.

"If I answer your questions, they'll kill me."

"I will make a deal with you. You can have a choice, I can send you back down to the pit where Satan will deal with you or I can send you up to Heaven for Jesus to deal with you. Whatever your choice, I will do it after you answer my questions."

"Send me to the Nazarene," he said. The three pulled his noose tighter immediately.

"I told you not to speak of Him like that! He is the King! Say it!"

"He is the King of the world!" He replied aggressively.

"He is much more than that," I said quietly. "Now tell me what your name is."

"Murder and hatred," he said shaking. "You know my name."

"And what is your assignment?"

"I can't tell you!"

"Who invited you here?"

"She did!" He pointed to the young girl who's only job was to become holy. She was still kneeling, head still bowed. I was shocked.

"Why?" I asked tenderly to her.

She looked up with hatred burning in her eyes. "How dare you say that to me in front of all these people!" I had embarrassed her by not giving her a job and telling her to be more holy.

I looked back at the demon for some answers. He responded, "She is without covering. Anyone who is without covering is subject to be my prey. Anyone that does not call you captain on this boat is my subject."

"You will have no subjects here!" I said back to him, even though I understood the law he was referring to. I had sinned greatly by not wanting anyone to call me that. It was false humility and I needed to take my place. "Tell me your assignment!"

He breathed in a gulp of air, knowing he had already gone too far and there was no going back now. "The plan was to murder the infants."

"What infants? The children?" I said in horror. The two kids emerged from the galley door that was opened and toddled in between the demon and I with no idea. They were playing with a kite and a wagon of blocks and were totally unaware of what was going on. I was furious and frightened at them all at the same time.

The demon looked at them as if he wanted to eat them alive. "No... I cannot even come near them. It is the infant intercessors I am after. Like her..." He motioned toward the one who had brought him here. "I have come to murder their calling and then murder yours. I will do it by the flesh if I have to, but I prefer the torture of the death of a spirit."

I looked back at the young girl who had caused all of this. I grabbed hold of her head and yelled, "In the name of Jesus, demon come out!" I then knelt at her feet, knowing the battle was not over, hearing the exhausted breaths of the demon in front of me.

"Please forgive me! Forgive me!" I pleaded to her softly. "I should not have done it that way. I should have whispered in your ear." I had known when I lay hands on her that she was an adulteress. I had no patience for that. I had also knew that she was expecting a word from me about how wonderful and chosen she was and that she was about to receive a worldwide ministry. I had been very annoyed by that. Here I was pleading at her feet, knowing the only way to get rid of this horrible thing was her forgiveness of me. I looked up and her hatred vanished. She looked soft, like a different person.

I looked up into her eyes. I had noticed that someone, probably Sean, had snuck my sword beside me. "You have to finish this," I whispered to her. "This is your battle, you have to be the one to kill this thing." She shook her head no. "Take my sword..." I said slowly and softly.

"I can't do it, Amy!" She cried. "Do it for me!"

I grabbed my sword and jolted into the under chin of the demon in less than a millisecond. I then started to twist. I was twisting his brain with my sword. I was confusing him so that he couldn't return. "Remember your promise..." he said with his eyes rolled back.

"You demons ask for mercy where you give none. Go up to Jesus for Him to deal with you!" He flew straight up in a flash, leaving the flesh carcass on the deck.

"What are we going to do with this?" Sean asked.

"He used a carcass. This person was already dead he inhabited. But still, this body has been exposed to this poison. I do not want the Lord's ocean touching any of this contamination. Get a tarp and seal him up and then throw him overboard." They found a huge, black tarp that sealed around. It was a body bag that was totally air proof. The Lord had expected this and provided for it.

CHAPTER 19

PAPERWORK

I went back to my cabin. I was tired. When I opened the door, I saw the young woman I had asked to come back here. I felt like just shooing her away. She was grinning, seemingly oblivious, and I could not disappoint her. I just couldn't minister yet. I sat down beside her and breathed in deeply. What came out was a huge burst of sobbing. I buried my face in my hands and then turned my head to the back wall where a small, elongated window was.

"It's okay, Amy, it's okay..." She soothed me like my best friend at home. How I missed her at this moment. A word came to me about her, *my helper*. How I needed one right then!

"I'm just so overwhelmed..." I whined.

"You're fine." She was confident. I peered out the little window. The only other window was a large one on the door. I hated the window on the door. It felt like such a violation of privacy. "I'm an angel..." she said.

"I know," I said right away, realizing it only seconds before.

"You are very dearly loved in Heaven, Amy." That statement meant so much to me. She stroked my back. "We have some paper work to do now." She produced an enormous stack of papers and placed a pair of spectacles on her face. It seemed funny to see an angel with glasses. I think they were just part of the costume.

"Why are you in that particular body?" I asked. She seemed oddly out of place. She was well over six feet tall and was built more like a large man. She seemed very young with dark, brown hair.

She laughed a little, "Because all of my other bodies were at the cleaners." I laughed, too. She continued, "Now, I know this is going to be difficult, but there's some unforgiveness you need to deal with..." I felt like I was going to throw up. God was not giving me any kind of slack that day!

"You have very good cases here. All of them seem very feasible to win in a court of law. These were just hideous things that were done to you. You have rights. You can hold onto this unforgiveness." But the Lord wouldn't allow that at all. I had given up my rights long ago.

I nodded for her to begin. A fire appeared at our feet. It took up the whole floor of the cabin. I moved my feet away instinctively. "Oh it's alright," she said, "the Lord told you that the only things here that could not be burned up is love. So you will be fine." I felt like that was a great compliment.

She took the top sheet of paper and handed it to me. On it was a very legal looking document. I scanned it quickly. It was a wretched account of something someone did to me during the death of someone very close to me. The actual sin was bold face, surrounded by regular type showing the atmosphere in which it was done in.

She shook her head. "What I find interesting, Amy, is that the majority of papers in this stack have to do with terrible things that happened to you right after a relative's death. You know, the spirit of correction does not come from the Lord if it is when you are grieving. The spirit of healing comes when you are grieving." She paused while I threw the paper into the fire. I looked at her fearfully.

"Are you the spirit of correction?" I asked meekly.

"Yes." She showed me her enormous hands. "But these hands are not so large so that they will knock you down. They are here to lift you up. Most of these things have already been dealt with in secret with you and the Holy Spirit over the passed six months. This is the formality of it all. Don't worry. The Lord may forget all of these sins that were done to you, but He never forgets to heal you from them. You must forgive, though, before He can get to you."

She continued, "Another one done fresh after a death..."

I looked at the account and then kissed the page. She gasped. "May I add to this one? The people who did this to me, will God not only forgive them, but save them as well?" She nodded, looking astonished.

"This one will be difficult. Another very difficult death during this one as well..." I looked at the page. "That person has a stack..."

"Throw them all in, every last one!"

"Even this one?" She handed me one that shot through my bones with pain.

"Even this one?" I threw them in the fire. The angel started crying. One by one they went until we neared the end, one painful memory after another.

"This is your husband. Lots of just little things with this one..." I flipped through them and tossed them in the fire as well.

There was only one page left. "Okay, just this one left." She looked up at me, red-eyed from crying. "I just have to ask you a question. Why is this so easy for you to forgive all these people?" This was not easy. This was at least six months of work, if not more she was looking at, piled neatly in a stack.

"You are an angel, so you do not understand. I have hurt others just like these people have hurt me and the Lord has forgiven me." She nodded.

"Okay, just this one, it should be the easiest. It's really rather almost humorous. This one is a list of all the things you haven't forgiven yourself for..."

I grabbed the list from her hand and folded it twice. "No, the Lord will keep this. I do not want this thrown in the fire, send it back to Him."

She looked at me in horror. "He has asked you to deal with this."

"I can't forgive myself."

She put her hands on my shoulders. "Forgive yourself because I love you! Forgive yourself because the Lord loves you."

"You don't understand, I have to forgive myself because I love me. And that's not something that I have right now."

"You have to do this, Amy, or the Lord will not come to you."

"God give me strength..." I whispered and threw it in the fire. She smiled at me and vanished.

The Lord appeared, sitting beside me on my left. My dress turned from red to topaz blue to represent grace. I looked at Him sitting there so still. I was exhausted. He motioned for me to lay in His arms. I leaned over next to Him as He silently wrapped His arm around my own.

THE PELTING RAIN

I awoke, it seemed, only a second later. He was gone and I was on my side, laying on the white cushions. A young man burst in my cabin. "Captain! We're taking on water!"

A small wave of water sloshed in with a fish on it's side sliding in with it.

"God, I don't want to be the captain," I moaned to Him. I walked out calmly and surveyed the scene. Storms I knew. This one was bad. The rain pelted down so hard that I could hardly see a thing. The water was sloshing all on the deck as the crew folded the sails down, trying not to lose their balance. When all the work was complete, I yelled for them all to go down below. Sean ushered them in and stayed there with them leaving me alone.

I needed to be on deck. There were many reasons, each of which difficult to explain. I wanted to see what we were up against, firstly. I wanted to know the winds, the amount of rain and how high the waves were. But, there was something far bigger than the responsibilities of captain. I *wanted* to be in the storm. Storms are pain, yes, but storms I crave. Until this passed season, all I had known was one storm after another. The relationship I had with the Master was one of clinging to Him. My job was to keep breathing. I actually missed those times of desperation. I knew He was in every rain drop, so I kept my balance in the middle of the deck and *felt* every drop I could. If He was the sun, I wanted to feel that radiance. If He was the hard rain, I wanted to feel His sharpness on my shoulders.[88]

The mast behind me was suddenly hit by lightning and actually split in two. This did not deter me. The waves threw the ship around as if it was weightless, but I knew where I was. I was in the City of God and He was in everything here. Something spiritual happened that day, standing there alone in the storm. I became the captain.

THE SONG

The waves kept rolling, but the storm suddenly stopped, revealing a beautiful, windy day again. The crew came out from below. I greeted each one with affection. My dress had turned into a uniform. I was wearing a cobalt blue uniform with a captain's hat to match.

"Let's clean up!" I barked the orders to the relieved crew.

"Should I go get the cd player?" One asked. It struck me as such a funny question, taking lot of where we were.

"We don't need it here. Let's ask the angels to accompany us," I said, smiling, excited for them all to hear first hand the song of Heaven. The waves seemed to be stringed instruments as they rose up and down, lifting us with their music. Then, from Heaven, we could hear the beautiful sound of the angels singing. They sang:

"Tell us of your love.
Tell us who He is!
Oh most beautiful of women!"[89]

They were asking all of us to tell them who God was to us. They longed for our revelation. Then, I heard the Lord, Himself, sing, "Tell me My name!"

Spontaneously, a song came up from the ship. Out of every crew member came a different tune. When it intertwined together, it was a wonderful, high melody. Each person sang who He was to them. One sang, "He's my Redeemer!"[90]

Another, "He's my friend!"

Another, "He's my Healer!" And on it went. I listened until the last one had joined in the song.

Then it was my turn. I sang out, my hands spread, my face to the sky, "YOU ARE BEAUTIFUL!" [91] And with that

I understood. With every storm, He teaches us one of His names. We learn a new name for Him from every storm.

CHAPTER 20

GRADUATION DAY

I stood and breathed deeply. My uniform was already drying up. The waves went back down and the day was beautiful again. *What now?* I asked myself and the Lord. I heard a cry come from the mast area above. Although the lightning had split it in two, the parts that were left up were the functioning ones. The part laying on it's side was just a hunk of the wood beam. I winced to look up. One of our guys had a telescope in his hand and was waving rapidly. "Land a'hoy!" He yelled to all of us.

Land? Land? What could this be– another island to visit? I looked, myself, and there were huge buildings along the banks. *Port! We were at a port. This couldn't be our port, though. This was way too fast.*

"Keep going!" I yelled to the crew who looked at me in horror.

"How do you know this is not the port?" The young man asked as he crawled down the mast.

"I don't but we can u-turn if I am wrong," I said as I withdrew to my cabin.

I removed my cap and brushed back my hair as I opened the door. I yelped in excitement when I saw Jesus sitting in my quarters! I threw myself at Him! I pulled back realizing the impact of this joyous meeting. I had seen Him here, yes, but not like this. He seemed His old self and He was so happy. "I'm done aren't I?" My eyes twinkled with the hope.

"You're done here," He said happily. I squealed with delight.

"Port! We've got to pull into port," I said, then pulled back to Him. "They can wait to hear the orders, we can always u-turn." He nodded. "I just want to be with You right now!" I said as I hugged Him again and again. He pulled me away, looked at me, then showered me with little kisses all over my face.

"I'm so happy that you succeeded," He told me exuberantly.

"But it was so short!" I retorted in reference to the length of time I was on the boat.

"Short? Short! I couldn't *wait* to see you again like this and you call it short!" I was happy He was actually thinking the same thing as me. We laughed and hugged.

We got up to leave about three or four times, only to find ourselves loving on each other again. Either I would pull Him back to me or He would pull me back when I started to get up to leave.

As we left, I noticed that there were shelves under the seats in my cabin. It was odd that I hadn't noticed them before. They were stuffed with games and even some knitting supplies. I asked the Lord about it and He said that I would be surprised how many captains have tried to fill up their time with that stuff instead of spending time with the Lord. I couldn't imagine it during this season.

Finally we left. With thrilled faces, we emerged to find the entire crew in line on the deck with huge, anticipatory smirks on their faces. The boat turned around toward the port when they saw us. The Lord and I were hand in hand when I cried out gleefully, "At ease!" They were all so giddy.

They crowded around the Lord who gave affection to all of them. Some of them had never seen Him before, so it was very emotional. He never let go of my hand the whole time. In fact, I could feel His thumb rubbing my hand, as if to say, "I'm still thinking about you, even though I'm giving attention to all these people."

My husband, Sean, came over to me. We kissed each other twice. "Come with me when we arrive at port," I asked him, knowing there would be a celebration of my arrival.

"No, hon'. This is your moment, not mine. You've earned it," he said. I smiled at him.

PORT

The crew was wiping tears away as we felt the thud of the dock on the side of the ship. I had dressed in a beautiful white dress. The Lord smiled at me and took my hand. A huge bridge was attached to the dock and our ship so that we could walk off. There was a crowd of people– about one thousand, cheering. There was confetti being thrown so much that it looked like it was snowing colored paper. We began to make our descent.

Half-way down I noticed something horrific. Toward the left of the bridge, close to the water and close to the crowd was a man. He was stripped to his waist and was being whipped. The torturer held a cigar in his mouth and was more interested in the festivities of our landing than if he was aiming correctly on the man.

I stopped and showed the Lord what was happening. He saw the man and instantly the whip was thrown out of the other man's hand and flew straight up. The Lord rushed to his side with me falling close behind. The Lord took a hold of the man who had been beaten severely and we walked him back onto the boat. The crowd already started dissipating, unhappy with the anti-climatic entrance we were performing.

The crew was put into action immediately. They surrounded the three of us. The Lord sent some of them to fetch supplies to help the man. The Lord sat close to the man on the bench. I sat on the other side of the Lord. The man was completely bald, probably in his fifties, and seemed to be very fit for his age. A silver bowl with some green liquid, I assumed was aloe, [92] and a clean cloth were brought to the Lord. As the man talked, the Lord very gently dabbed his wounds.

He told us through tears how he had ministered to the people that lived in this town. This is how they repaid him. The Lord whispered to me quietly, "He's the planter, you are the harvester. You've come to harvest what he's bled for." [93] I wanted so badly for the man to stay and help us harvest, but he was not in good shape and desperately needed some ministering to.

When the Lord had finished putting the medicine on him, he started stroking his back with the cloth. With each stroke, the wounds came off as if they were put on by a makeup artist in a movie. The man was completely healed. The funny thing was, he didn't think it was out of the ordinary. He just continued to talk softly and slowly.

"Do you want to come back with Me?" The Lord asked the man gently. He was giving him the option to stay. The man immediately shook his head yes. A small group of gentle women on board took the man back to my cabin to rest. I doubted if the Lord was coming with me as well until He assured me He was. The crew's purpose was to minister to this very exhausted missionary. They were going to take Him back to the city to be refreshed. How I wanted to go, too!

But, here was my calling in front of me. We got up again and started walking down the platform to the town again.

The people had pulled back and gone back to their houses. They were not pleased at all that we had honored this man they were torturing. Angels filed in instead to greet us. You could see the people parting from the port and the angels coming. It was like watching the parting of the Red Sea.

We smiled at each other and watched as the angels erupted in cheer. It was even more exuberant than before. The praise of men is not something that I wanted. I was actually on the watch for it because it didn't mean I was doing the right thing. It usually meant the opposite. But, here were the angels– the angels knew this was good. I walked down to my new place.

THE TOWN

Sean and our children walked off the boat as well and stayed in the crowd of angels as we slipped passed them and went into the center of town. I blew a kiss to my crew who was smiling and looking on from the deck. I took a look at the town. It looked like London during Columbus' times. There were tall apartment-like buildings that were flat in the front. There were all dirt roads that had an orange tint to them and seemed muddy. "Why have I come here?" I asked the Lord.

"You are going to build a well here," I looked around.

"Here?" I asked. He turned towards me and smiled.

"Do you love me [right] here?"

"Yes."

"Then this is a perfect place to build a well." He crouched down. I saw a well being dug and built in front of Him in seconds.

"Lord, I want to build wells where others outside the town gates can drink." He nodded in approval.

A dozen children came running out of a few flats towards us. They pulled at my white dress, wanting attention. I freely gave it. They were so adorable. "You're pretty," one little girl said.

I was a little taken back by this comment, but I quickly recovered and said, "Go tell *Him.* He made me!" I motioned her to Jesus standing a few steps from me. They all rushed over to Him and the little girl immediately caught His attention as well.

"Make me pretty, too!" she chimed.

He laughed, "You are already pretty. But I will continue to make you more so." She seemed pleased with this answer.

Her mood swung serious. "I know why our parents do not want to see Amy."

"Why?" I asked.

"Because they didn't want you to help the man they were hurting."

"Why were they hurting the man?"

"Because he told them they have to live pure," she said. After a long pause, she added, "They keep slaves here..." Both of our antennas went up. No wonder the ship was a slave ship at one time. This was a port of call. I looked at the Lord in horror.

"Where are they?" The Lord asked hurriedly.

THE CAPTURED ONES

"I will show you..." The Lord put the little girl down and she led us about one hundred feet away where trees started. There was a round sewage lid on the ground. We lifted it up. The Lord went first. We climbed down a small ladder into the underground area. The light of the Lord shown all around. It seemed to be an eerie orange color that lit everything up.

I gasped. There were people– slaves– handcuffed to the ceiling. There were also some who were belted to the ceiling. They looked like their owners had taken their own belts off and used those to shackle them. Sewage leaked into the area like disgusting waterfalls.

"Give me the revelation on this, Lord," I prayed.

He began, "The people in the town represents the people in the church. These people are the ones that the church has rejected. The church has chained them down here and caused them to believe there is no escape; that there is no forgiveness. They have sometimes come down here, gotten one of them, used them, and then returned them again." I wanted to cry bitterly, but knew I couldn't. This was horrific.

"I am the Key!" [94] He proclaimed to me and all the others. He took a key out of His pocket and began unlocking their shackles. I started unbelting the ones that were belted. As we worked, I watched the Lord. He finally turned around and said, "Pay attention to who you are freeing."

I looked back at the person I was releasing. She was a very old woman with almost no teeth. She had wrinkles everywhere and was hunched over. When I saw her, I knew she didn't have the strength to make it out of that place. "Don't worry. We will carry you. He is very strong."

"Yes!" She said, "He is very strong!" As she proclaimed it, six demons flew out of her and were absorbed into the soft-coated ceiling. I carried her out of the hole. She winced in the light around the town. I sped with her around my shoulders. I was going towards the boat. She smelled terrible.

I set her down at the dock. I could barely see the ship, it had already launched. A young man was cleaning his small boat by the dock and I called to him. I gave him a sack of money which appeared miraculously. I told him to hurry and take her to the boat. She looked at me. She was afraid he would throw her off the boat when he got out further, just so he wouldn't have to work hard to get her to the ship. I looked around at the crowd of angels, still socializing by the dock. I assigned one of the female angels to her and had her go with her.

When she was safely out to sea, I hurried back to the hole and climbed down again in my white dress. The Lord was almost done freeing everyone. There were only a small few who were released that did not want to come with us. With those, He told them that the door would be open for them if they changed their mind. And, oh, how He hoped they would change their mind!

When the last was free, they all just stood there for a second. Then, the whole place erupted with a song of praise! It sounded like a style of music I had never heard before. It was a lot like African music. They sang, "We are free! We are the freed ones!"

THE CRUSADE

At last, He began to lead them all out. They filed out single file with me as the lead and the Lord bringing up the rear. They were a motley crew. Most were half naked and filthy sweaty. Their clothes were more like rags and they smelled so of the sewer they had lived in.

Just a few feet from the mouth of the hole, something miraculous had happened. An outdoor stadium had been built within just a few minutes. The group of angels who had greeted us had built and organized the whole event unfolding in front of our eyes. It was a crusade!

I led my team of castaways to the stadium where they took their seats on fold-up chairs on a lawn. Thousands were on the bleachers all around. The air was electric with music and excitement. Along with our band of freed slaves, there were people of all race and nationality all around. Most were dressed casually, but some were dressed to the hilt.

I took my spot on the stage. I had no idea what I was doing. The Lord sat close like a mother of a toddler performing on stage. I looked at Him for cues. He got up every few minutes to whisper the line I was suppose to say in my ear. I was relieved, because I had no idea what to say.

After a while, He came up to me and whispered, "Lay hands on the sick, Amy. I will heal every one of them without exception." I nodded. I had really never done that before. I looked at Him with saucer eyes as the stadium waited for my every move. He got up, patiently again, seeing my agony and stood next to me. He fashioned my hands so that my palms were facing down. He had the angels begin to move those with a need to the stage.

He put His hands over my hands and pushed gently. The feeling that went through my hands onto the people who I was laying hands on was a wonderful experience. It felt like soft electricity. It wasn't sharp or painful, it was like a soothing energy that passed through me unto the people.

It did start to feel like we were encountering opposition, however. Everything I did felt strained and the people were losing interest, oddly enough. Suddenly, the sprinkler system turned on! The entire grassy field had a timer that turned the sprinkler on. People were screaming and trying to get out of the way. I was soaked and so was the majority of the thousands of people. This was a good thing, however, for the freedmen. They were joyful. The stench coming from them drained away and they were cleaned up. I'm sure it felt good to them.

However, the ones who had come from town, dressed to the hilt, were absolutely exasperated. It made me want to laugh as they angrily shook their hands to wave off some of the water they were drenched in. They filed out, leaving only roughly half of the original audience. When everything calmed down and the sprinklers had finally stopped, the air felt fresh and alive. The people were swimming in joy. It was beautiful to see. All eyes went back on me and I continued laying hands on the people with the Lord firmly at my side.

He said to me as we were going, "One day, it will feel like you are floating above your body as all of this is going on. *I will be doing all of it.*" I smiled at Him, hardly believing any of what I was seeing or He what He was saying. When will the Bride do all of this? When will they minister to every tribe? When will they know who they are?

After only a little while, I stopped and looked at Him. I felt like something was over. I began to fill up with tears. "This is it, isn't it?" I asked softly.

He shook His head yes. Then He brushed His hand on my face and said, "Yes. But for you, My love, it is only the beginning of a great adventure."

ENDNOTES

1. Honey- Psalm 81:16 speaks of God wanting to give this to the Israelites to eat. "...And with honey from the rock I would have satisfied you." Psalm 19:10 also speaks of the judgements of the Lord as "... Sweater also than honey and the honeycomb."

2. Song of Solomon 2:10 "My beloved spoke, and said to me: Rise up, my love, my fair one, And come away."

3. Song of Solomon 3: 2: "I will rise now," *I said*, "And go about the city; in the streets and in the squares I will seek the one I love." I sought him, but I did not find him. The watchmen who go about the city found me; I said, "Have you seen the one I love?"

4. The honey also represented renewal like what Jesus ate after the resurrection (Luke 24: 42). The pomegranates represented ministering to the Lord because the Priests would wear them on the hem of their garments.

5. 1 Chronicles 11 :11

6. You will see this illustration repeated a lot. Genesis 37:3 "Now Israel loved Joseph... he made him a tunic of many colors."

7. Hebrew 13:5

8. Song of Solomon 3:4

9. Psalm 40:1-2 "I waited patiently for the Lord; He inclined to me, And heard my cry. He also brought me up out of a horrible pit, Out of the miry clay, And set my feet upon a rock, *And* established my steps."

10. Song of Solomon 8:6 "Set me upon your heart, As a seal upon your arm..."

11. Priestly garments. Exodus 39:1, 25, 26

12. Genesis 3:21

13. Song of Solomon 4:1

14. Song of Solomon 1:17 "The beams of our house are cedar." 1 Kings 6:18 "The inside of the temple was cedar..."

15. Song of Solomon 5: 10-13, 16

16. Ephesians 6:15

17. Song of Solomon 2:16

18. Revelation 4:3

19. John 20-21 "I do not pray for these alone, but also for those who will believe in Me through their word; that

they all may be one, as You, Father, *are* in Me and I in You; that they also may be one in Us that the world may believe that You sent Me."

20. 1 John 4:18 "There is no fear in love; but perfect love casts out fear, because fear involves torment. But he who fears has not been made perfect in love."

21. Psalm 46:4

22. Genesis 28:12

23. Revelation 4

24. Romans 8:15

25. John 21:17

26. John 20: 27

27. 2 Samuel tells of David's cave and castle experiences

28. Over and over in scripture we see the Lord giving exact battle plans. (e.g. Gideon's valiant three hundred in the book of Judges.)

29. Malachi 4:2 Healing in His wings

30. The tree here shows the Lord as a refuge. There are many in trouble here, perishing in their sin, the Bride here is shown spiritually pushing them to safety.

31. Each of the individuals would move from the point of salvation to the point of servant-hood.

32. Again, another image of Joseph's coat of many colors. It shows being chosen for a special purpose.

33. Throughout the dream, I change clothes again and again. This imagery is to teach that we change with each new revelation given to us in our walk. We even will look different as we learn more.

34. The waterfall signifies the refreshing of the relationship between the Bride and the Lord.

35. "The River is Here" By Andy Park, 1994 Mercy Publishing.

36. "Fairest Lord Jesus" Public Domain. By Munster Gesangbuch, Translated by Joseph August Seiss

37. Matthew 17:27

38. John 3:30

39. 2 Samuel 24:24

40. 1 Samuel 17:40 shows David having 5 small stones. Although not seemingly powerful weapons, one was all God needed to defeat the giant.

41. Romans 6:11

42. Ezekiel 1: 15-20

43. Revelation 4:8

44. Ezekiel 4

45. Ezekiel 3: 17-20

46. This information is a traditional view point of Ezekiel's death– that he was killed by the other exiles.

47. 2 Peter 3:8

48. Exodus 20: 3

49. The story of David can be found in 2 Samuel

50. Quote from "Cinderella" Copyright the Walt Disney Company 1950

51. Philippians 4:4

52. Isaiah 11: 6-9

53. Revelation 19:11

54. Matthew 11:27 Shows that Jesus reveals the Father

55. 1 Chronicles 4: 10

56. John 4: 14

57. Hebrews 13:5

58. Genesis 3: 15

59. Romans 8: 26

60. Matthew 18: 3-4

61. 1 Kings 6: 29

62. 1 Samuel 3: 3-4

63. Matthew 27: 51

64. Description of the Arc can be found in Exodus 25: 10-22

65. Luke 13:34 Shows one of the times the Lord interceded for Jerusalem

66. Revelation 5:5

67. Matthew 11: 29-30

68. Revelation 22:16

69. Revelation 4:10

70. John 19:30

71. This was a difficult statement to interpret. The author believes that the Lord is comforting her and showing her that because of His great love between He and His church, the pain was easier to take.

72. John 21: 7

73. Philippians 1:21

74. Philippians 1: 29

75. Patmos is an island in which John was banished and forced to serve in the mines. It is a barren place.

76. The wells are significant of the knowledge and full-ness of God. When we drink deeply of Him, we gain new insight into His wonderful nature. Our spirits are also refreshed here by His presence. These people were trying to be refreshed and gain life through the world. They each had gods that were not giving them any life.

77. The treasure represent the gifts of the Spirit.

78. Isaiah 61:1 Is just one example of the Lord, our Healer

79. John 14:16 The word "Helper" can also be interpreted, "Comforter"

80. The "dislodger" is a person who brings in an anointing of forgiveness that allows the people who are "stuck" in sin to be free from the trappings of it. The dislodger is often an intercessor who specializes in warfare.
The "inspector" is usually called to counseling or internal healing, taking note of how the person was wounded by the sin and finding ways to healing.

81. The catcher of the food, here, is the role of the teacher

82. The person in charge of steering has an administrative anointing. This person leads and organizes a group of people in the direction they are to go.

83. The "dish keeper" here is a symbolic of the helps ministry. This is a broad- spectrum calling that can be from simply organizing an event to preparing the bulletin. It is an important role because they provide an atmosphere to learn and worship.

84. This is the role of the encourager. This person lifts up and beautifies the Church. He sheds light on the goodness that the Lord placed on the Church so that the lost will want what they have.

85. This position is one of accountability. This is usually a friend of the person– she makes sure that even the deepest feelings of the person line up with the Word.

86. The "cleaners" are the intercessors. They are the ones that the Holy Spirit imparts wisdom in to as to what needs to be prayed through. They often have divine insight as to where impurities lie so that they can pull them out.

87. The author wrote this journal entry a week before the Virginia Tech. shootings. She said that she heard the word, "murder" over twenty to thirty times. It is an interesting side-note.

88. The storm represents the difficulties and persecutions in life.

89. Even the angels desire new revelation of Him– their revelations of Him come from us. Song of Solomon 6: 1 "Where has your beloved gone, O fairest among women? Where has your beloved turned aside, that we may seek him with you?"

90. Job 19: 25 "For I know *that* my Redeemer lives, and He shall stand at last on the earth."

91. Psalm 27:4

92. Numbers 24: 6

93. John 4: 37-38

94. Isaiah 22:22 " The key of the house of David I will lay on His shoulder; So He shall open, and no one shall shut..."

ACKNOWLEDGMENTS

I would like to thank "the invisible warrior", my husband, Sean.

How can I thank Patricia Vonderembse enough who's life has deeply inspired mine, who's prayer life has kept me alive, and who's house I was at when this started.

A huge thank you goes to Albert and Anna Rountree for their book <u>Priestly Bride</u> which confirmed SOOO much to me of what the Spirit was showing!!!

I would also like to thank Terry MacAlmon who's songs continue to bring me into the arms of my Master.

And, especially, I thank my parents, Paul and Bonnie Fischle, who introduced me at a young age to the Love of my life.

Printed in the United States
87284LV00003B/52-99/A